What Your Colleagues Are Saying . . .

Simplifying STEM, PreK–5 addresses the challenge of persistent inequities in STEM education with an approach to teaching that draws strength from the complex ways in which identities, culture, and context intersect in the classroom and our world. Weaving theory and practice with rich classroom examples, this book unpacks with beautiful clarity inclusive and equitable approaches that value, cultivate, and leverage diverse perspectives and experiences so that meaningful learning is available for all!

Cathery Yeh
Assistant Professor of STEM Education
Core faculty for the Center for Asian American Studies
The University of Texas at Austin
Austin, TX

If you've been told that there either aren't enough or too many integrated STEM resources for practitioners, know that *Simplifying STEM, PreK–5* offers real-world examples that are complex yet accessible to all audiences. With "try this" teacher and scholar actions, the authors take novices to experts on an intellectual journey in STEM spaces. They weave information that further explains STEM in today's context that makes the reader excited to imagine as well as try something creative.

Andrea Borowczak
President of the Association of Science Teacher Educators
Director and Professor, School of Teacher Education
University of Central Florida
Orlando, FL

Simplifying STEM, PreK–5: Four Equitable Practices to Inspire Meaningful Learning provides a framework for teaching Integrated STEM Practices. It includes vignettes to show teachers how to integrate them into their lessons with grade-appropriate connections. I appreciate how the "So you've been told . . ." statements and "Reality Check!" responses throughout the chapters address many misconceptions and ideas educators confront.

Robert Q. Berry III
Past President of the National Council of Teachers of Mathematics
Dean of the College of Education
University of Arizona
Tucson, AZ

T0405977

Simplifying STEM seeks to de-center whiteness and disrupt the STEM status quo. Readers are provided practical examples and essential strategies that can be used in their respective environments to create inclusive STEM environments that give all scholars opportunities to be successful.

Kristopher J. Childs
CEO
K Childs Solutions
Winter Garden, FL

The authors of this text bring attention to the growing need of equity-centered STEM education that rightfully positions children and learners as the impetus for integrative STEM. As a former teacher and current educational researcher, I am deeply impressed by the suggestions and tasks that are offered in this text. All STEM teachers both new and veterans, need to read this book. It offers a critical examination of our practices and offers implementable suggestions to ensure that every student develops a sense of belonging in STEM.

Daniel Edelen
Assistant Professor of Elementary Mathematics Education
Georgia State University
Decatur, GA

A must-read to ensure equity and engagement for all elementary STEM learners. This book provides step-by-step, easy to implement strategies to encourage critical thinking, collaboration, and communication.

Virginia R. Jones
Past President, International Technology and Engineering Educators
Association
South Boston, VA

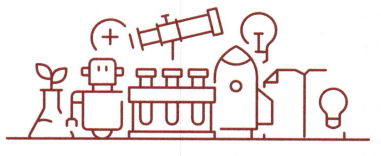

Simplifying
STEM

Grades PreK–5

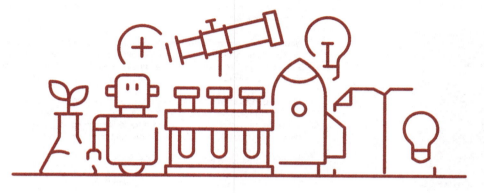

Simplifying
STEM

Four Equitable Practices to Inspire Meaningful Learning

Christa Jackson • Thomas Roberts • Cathrine Maiorca
Kristin L. Cook • Sarah B. Bush • Margaret Mohr-Schroeder
with Julie A. Sicks-Panus and Tracy Young

CORWIN

FOR INFORMATION:

Corwin

A SAGE Company

2455 Teller Road

Thousand Oaks, California 91320

(800) 233-9936

www.corwin.com

SAGE Publications Ltd.

1 Oliver's Yard

55 City Road

London EC1Y 1SP

United Kingdom

SAGE Publications India Pvt. Ltd.

Unit No 323-333, Third Floor, F-Block

International Trade Tower Nehru Place

New Delhi 110 019

India

SAGE Publications Asia-Pacific Pte. Ltd.

18 Cross Street #10-10/11/12

China Square Central

Singapore 048423

Vice President and
   Editorial Director: Monica Eckman

Associate Director and
   Publisher, STEM: Erin Null

Acquisitions Editor: Debbie Hardin

Senior Editorial Assistant: Nyle De Leon

Production Editor: Tori Mirsadjadi

Copy Editor: Gillian Dickens

Typesetter: C&M Digitals (P) Ltd.

Proofreader: Barbara Coster

Indexer: Integra

Cover Designer: Gail Buschman

Marketing Manager: Margaret O'Connor

Printed in the United States of America

Library of Congress Cataloging-in-Publication Data

Names: Jackson, Christa, author. | Roberts, Thomas, author. | Maiorca, Cathrine, author. | Cook, Kristin Leigh., author. | Bush, Sarah B., author. | Mohr-Schroeder, Margaret J., author.

Title: Simplifying STEM grades PreK-5 : four equitable practices to inspire meaningful learning / Christa Jackson, Thomas Roberts, Cathrine Maiorca, Kristin L. Cook, Sarah B. Bush, Margaret J. Mohr-Schroeder with Julie A. Sicks-Panus and Tracy Young.

Description: Thousand Oaks, California : Corwin, [2024] | Series: Corwin mathematics series | Includes bibliographical references and index.

Identifiers: LCCN 2023051977 | ISBN 9781071917053 (paperback) | ISBN 9781071932315 (epub) | ISBN 9781071932322 (epub) | ISBN 9781071932339 (pdf)

Subjects: LCSH: Curriculum planning. | Interdisciplinary approach in education. | Science—Study and teaching (Kindergarten) | Science—Study and teaching (Elementary) | Technology—Study and teaching (Kindergarten) | Technology—Study and teaching (Elementary)

Classification: LCC LB2806.15 .J275 2024 | DDC 375/.001—dc23/eng/20231129

LC record available at https://lccn.loc.gov/2023051977

This book is printed on acid-free paper.

24 25 26 27 28 10 9 8 7 6 5 4 3 2 1

CONTENTS

CHAPTER 2: ISP 1: USE CRITICAL AND CREATIVE THINKING TO SEEK SOLUTIONS — 25

CHAPTER 3: ISP 2: COLLABORATE AND USE APPROPRIATE TOOLS TO ENGAGE IN ITERATIVE DESIGN — 48

CHAPTER 4: ISP 3: COMMUNICATE SOLUTIONS BASED ON EVIDENCE AND DATA

CHAPTER 5: ISP 4: RECOGNIZE AND USE STRUCTURES IN REAL-WORLD SYSTEMS 96

CHAPTER 6: REIMAGINING EXISTING STEM TASKS 121

Visit the companion website at
qrs.ly/s9f1lux
for downloadable resources.

LIST OF ACRONYMS USED THROUGHOUT THE BOOK

CAD: Computer-aided design

CCSSO: Council of Chief State School Officers

CER: Claims, evidence, reasoning

CNC: Computer numerical control

ISP: Integrated STEM Practices

ITEEA: International Technology and Engineering Educators Association

NCTM: National Council of Teachers of Mathematics

NGSS: Next Generation Science Standards

PGM: People of global majority

SEP: Science and Engineering Practices

SMP: Standards for Mathematical Practices

STEL: Standards for Technological and Engineering Literacy

STEM: Science, Technology, Engineering, and Mathematics

TEP: Technology and Engineering Practices

PREFACE

Simplifying STEM: Four Equitable Practices to Inspire Meaningful Learning is a book born from our collective work in integrated STEM. Integrated STEM uses multiple STEM disciplines to collaboratively seek solutions to challenges faced in our communities, region, country, and even the world with the ultimate goal of increasing scholars' STEM literacy. To ensure integrated STEM actively positions each scholar as a valuable member of the STEM community, we center our work in the Equity-Oriented Conceptual Framework for STEM Literacy (Jackson et al., 2021), which provides opportunity and access to all scholars, especially those who have been historically excluded in STEM, to participate in high-quality integrated STEM learning experiences. High-quality STEM learning experiences provide scholars an opportunity to apply the content and practices when seeking solutions to challenges in our world that are meaningful and interesting to them. When scholars have access to these high-quality integrated STEM learning experiences, this helps to develop positive STEM identities and productive dispositions as they use reasoning and sense-making to apply ideas from STEM subjects. The high-quality STEM learning experiences provide authentic opportunities (Roberts & Chapman, 2017) for scholars to apply discipline-specific content in rigorous ways (Jackson et al., 2021). This often occurs through the engagement in the Integrated STEM Practices (ISPs) (Roberts et al., 2022). Because state content standards in science, technology, engineering, and mathematics are not generally aligned to integrated STEM initiatives (Bybee, 2018), a coherent set of integrated STEM practices is needed. It is through this need that we have collectively written this book. It is through our broader STEM commitment that we can transform STEM instruction to empower the next generation to be societal change agents.

While the predominant focus of this book is not on describing an array of high-quality STEM learning experiences, we draw upon high-quality STEM learning experiences to describe the ISPs evident within the STEM learning experience. As you read and engage with the book, you will experience what high-quality STEM experiences look like, sound like, and feel like in the classroom. You will take away several high-quality STEM learning experiences that you can adapt and use in your instruction as well as take your own STEM learning experiences and recenter them to focus on the ISPs. More important, though, you'll leave with a vision for implementing the ISPs in ways that are contextually responsive to your scholars, your school, and your community.

ACKNOWLEDGMENTS

We would like to thank the teachers who have allowed us to use their instructional practice to create the stories for Chapters 2–5 to introduce each Integrated STEM Practice.

Publisher's Acknowledgments

Corwin gratefully acknowledges the contributions of the following reviewers:

Virginia R. Jones
Past President
International Technology and Engineering Educators Association
South Boston, VA

Megan Burton
Past President
Association of Mathematics Teacher Educators
Professor of Elementary Mathematics and STEM Education
Auburn University
Auburn, AL

ABOUT THE AUTHORS

 **Dr. Christa Jackson,** a former elementary and middle school mathematics and science teacher, is a Professor of Mathematics, Science, and STEM Education at Saint Louis University. She is the Founder and Director of the Institute for STEM Collaboration, Outreach, Research, and Education (iSCORE), where she focuses on transforming the STEM community one mind at a time through fostering scholars' STEM literacy development, STEM identities, and STEM sense of belonging. Dr. Jackson researches the development, use, and implementation of integrated STEM curriculum as well as understands the influence curricular materials and the related standards have on teachers' practices and the opportunities the curricular materials afford scholars to engage in STEM. Dr. Jackson served as a lead writer for *Catalyzing Change in Middle School Mathematics: Initiating Critical Conversations.* She recently completed her term as President of the School Science and Mathematics Association (SSMA) (2020–2022). Dr. Jackson is a professional developer and a mathematics and STEM consultant who has provided workshops to local, regional, national, and international communities.

Dr. Thomas Roberts, a former elementary school teacher, is an Associate Professor and co-program coordinator of the Inclusive PreK–5 Education Program at Bowling Green State University, where he teaches STEM education and mathematics education courses. He received his doctorate in Education Sciences specializing in STEM Education from the University of Kentucky. Dr. Roberts's research explores students' perceptions of STEM learning environments and ways to increase the effectiveness of teachers' instructional practices so that all students have the opportunity to participate in high-quality STEM learning. He is the Editor in Chief of *Technology and Engineering Education*, a peer-reviewed practitioner journal for integrated STEM teachers published by the International Technology and Engineering Educators Association (ITEEA).

Dr. Cathrine Maiorca, a former high school mathematics teacher, is an Assistant Professor of Mathematics Education at Oklahoma State University, where she teaches courses in mathematics education and STEM education. She received her doctorate in Curriculum and Instruction with an emphasis in Mathematics Education from the University of Nevada, Las Vegas. Dr. Maiorca's research interests include model-eliciting activities, effective STEM teaching and learning practices for every student, integrated STEM education in formal and informal settings, preservice teachers, and students' dispositions toward integrated STEM. Dr. Maiorca was an AMTE STaR fellow in 2018 and the 2020 School Science and Mathematics (SSMA) Early Career Scholar Award recipient. She is also an Associate Editor for *Technology and Engineering Education*, a peer-reviewed practitioner journal for integrated STEM teachers published by the International Technology and Engineering Educators Association (ITEEA).

Dr. Kristin L. Cook, a former high school science teacher, is a Professor of Science Education in the School of Education at Bellarmine University. She received her doctorate in Curriculum and Instruction specializing in Science Education and Environmental Sciences from Indiana University. Dr. Cook teaches courses in K–12 science methods and STEAM Education. In addition to teaching initial certification and advanced graduate classes, Dr. Cook serves as a professional developer and consultant for K–12 STEAM-focused school reform and project and problem-based learning development. Dr. Cook is actively involved in federal grants and research that focus on engaging students and teachers with the community of science through the exploration of socio-scientific inquiry and transdisciplinary STEAM instruction.

Dr. Sarah B. Bush, a former middle school mathematics teacher, is a Professor of K–12 STEM Education and the Lockheed Martin Eminent Scholar Chair at the University of Central Florida. At the University of Central Florida, she is the Director of the Lockheed Martin/ UCF Mathematics and Science Academy and is the program coordinator of the Mathematics Education PhD track. She teaches primarily graduate courses in mathematics education. She is a prolific writer who has authored 12 books and more than 100 journal articles and book chapters. Dr. Bush recently completed a term (2019–2022) as a member of the National Council of Teachers of Mathematics Board of Directors. She served as the lead writer and task force chair for NCTM's *Catalyzing Change in Middle School Mathematics: Initiating Critical Conversations.* Dr. Bush was the recipient of the 2021 School Science and Mathematics Association (SSMA) Award for Excellence in Integrating Science and Mathematics and 2018 recipient of the Association of Mathematics Teacher Educators (AMTE) Early Career Award. Dr. Bush seamlessly integrates her practical experience as a middle school mathematics teacher in public schools with her innovative scholarship to serve as an instructional leader in the field of mathematics education and STE(A)M education.

Dr. Margaret Mohr-Schroeder, is a Professor of STEM Education and Senior Associate Dean in the College of Education at the University of Kentucky (UK). She received her doctorate in curriculum and instruction specializing in mathematics and science education from Texas A&M University. Since her arrival at UK in 2006, she has been involved in over $17 million in federal and state funding, helping to expand research and broaden participation in STEM Education. She is a coeditor of the first *Handbook of Research on STEM Education* and coeditor of *STEM 2.0.* Her research interests include the transdisciplinary nature of STEM education and how they can be applied to innovative preservice teacher education and K–12 school models. Further, she investigates ways to broaden participation in STEM, especially for underrepresented populations and the effects these mechanisms have on their STEM literacy. Through this work, she has gained perspective on how to create opportunity and access to STEM activities to populations who normally would not have the opportunity and has witnessed and studied the significant impacts these mechanisms have. She is President of School Science and Mathematics Association, the world's oldest STEM organization.

Teacher Contributors

Ms. Julie A. Sicks-Panus is a K–8 STEM Specialist at Plymouth Elementary School.

Ms. Tracy Young is a STEM Specialist/Engineering by Design K–5 at Benton Hall Academy Little Falls City School District.

STEM ACROSS THE DISCIPLINES AS MUTUALLY SUPPORTIVE

Congratulations! If you're reading this book, you are on your way to start, focus, or extend your STEM journey. In this book, you will learn how to simplify STEM by using four equitable practices to inspire meaningful learning. This will transform your teaching as well as the lives of your scholars for both today and their future!

You likely know that the acronym STEM stands for **S**cience, **T**echnology, **E**ngineering, and **M**athematics. In the 1990s, the STEM acronym was first used by the National Science Foundation to describe projects, policies, programs, practices, and events related to one or a combination of the STEM disciplines (Bybee, 2010a, 2010b). Instead of focusing on individual STEM disciplines, we intentionally ground our practice within integrated STEM.

In this book, we define integrated STEM from an authentic interdisciplinary perspective. We view the STEM disciplines as being naturally intertwined and simultaneously needed to engage in STEM thinking to reach solutions for very real issues in our communities, nation, and the world. When applying content from multiple STEM disciplines, we don't mean that it must be all the STEM disciplines all the time but rather have the context to drive what STEM disciplines are needed to provide ideas or solutions.

You may have noticed that we refer to students as "scholars." We recognize that students have not yet achieved "scholar status" in the academic sense, but rather we refer to students as scholars to embody the empowering nature of adopting asset-based, equitable STEM teaching.

Stop, Think, Reflect (1A)

1. What does integrated STEM look, feel, and sound like?

2. What does it look like for scholars to do integrated STEM?

3. What does it look like for educators to facilitate integrated STEM?

4. Why should integrated STEM be implemented in our instructional practice?

 Available for download at **qrs.ly/s9f1lux**

Why Are Integrated STEM Learning Experiences Vital in PreK–12?

There is a critical need for PreK–12 high-quality and meaningful integrated STEM learning experiences. Every year, our society becomes more dependent on STEM content and process skills, thanks to a range of advances in technology, medical discoveries, big data, advanced mathematical modeling, computer science, artificial intelligence, advanced air mobility, and more—as well as a range of global challenges such as climate change, a global pandemic, growing cybersecurity threats, pollution, and so on. STEM occupations continue to grow at exponential rates, especially compared to non-STEM-based occupations. As of this writing in 2024, STEM occupations are projected to continue to increase by at least 11% over the next 10 years (Krutsch & Roderick, 2022). This growth is considered substantial because it's faster than the average growth rate for all occupations. It is important to remember that specific growth rates may vary for different STEM fields and regions. It's also important to recognize that STEM knowledge and skills are becoming increasingly valuable within any career and a necessity in our rapidly changing world, so providing scholars with a solid foundation in these areas can benefit them in numerous ways (Graf et al., 2018). But beyond the future jobs our scholars will fulfill in traditional STEM occupations, society now also relies heavily on scholars to take on jobs that are transdisciplinary (moves beyond the disciplines while at the same time respects disciplinary expertise to generate new knowledge) in nature and incorporate many facets of STEM such as innovators, designers, and creators. This necessity of transdisciplinary understanding of STEM holds for jobs that require a college degree as well as those that do not—for example, jobs in automobile manufacturing and repair have become increasingly technological as our automobiles are more dependent on computer technology and artificial intelligence.

Because of these future (and current) demands for STEM understanding and application, it is important for all scholars, regardless of whether they ultimately pursue a STEM career, to have access to and develop a strong sense of STEM literacy (Mohr-Schroeder et al., 2020). STEM literacy is essential to be an informed consumer and member of society. STEM literacy informs what we eat, what we buy, how we interact with our local community and the world, and how we seek solutions to real-world challenges we encounter. It is through the continual development of STEM literacy that scholars can collaborate, question, and engage in the utility of STEM concepts as they are challenged to provide solutions that cannot be readily solved using a single discipline (Bush & Cook, 2018). Approaching integrated STEM learning through rigor, discourse, and purpose can help scholars develop a deep understanding of discipline-specific content and how it can be applied in different contexts. This approach can also foster a sense of curiosity and a desire to learn more about STEM topics, which can lead to lifelong appreciation and interest in these areas.

Access to High-Quality Integrated STEM Education

Not everyone has had access to high-quality STEM education. Historically, STEM disciplines have been taught whole class with a value on right answers and little room for individuality or creativity. Integrated STEM curricula are still relatively new and, to implement well, can be cost prohibitive for schools and school districts to support. Thus, both through the way STEM disciplines are traditionally taught and the access teachers need to resources, including professional development, systemic barriers remain in place that maintain the STEM status quo (Love et al., 2017). As a result, the historical inequities many of our scholars continue to face in STEM are not new. Still further, much of the curriculum found in schools across the nation often does not consider the needs of their local communities (Bullock, 2017). It is time to completely change our approach to integrated STEM! It is essential that we provide all our scholars with meaningful opportunities and access to integrated STEM during PreK–12 to counter the racial, socioeconomic, regional, cultural, ability-centric, and gender inequities that exist within STEM. This commitment will empower all scholars to see that they are capable of doing STEM (Edelen & Bush, 2021). See Figure 1.1.

The National Research Council in 2011 established three goals for STEM education to address inequities, which include the following:

1. Expand the number of students who ultimately pursue advanced degrees and careers in STEM fields and broaden the participation of women and minorities in those fields.

2. Expand the STEM-capable workforce while broadening the participation of women and minorities.

3. Increase STEM literacy for all students, including those who do not pursue STEM-related careers or additional study in the STEM disciplines (pp. 4–5).

As educators, instructional coaches, leaders, and policymakers, we must ask ourselves what we can do to disrupt the STEM status quo and ensure we are providing high-quality integrated STEM learning experiences to all of our scholars. Through the years, data and research have pointed to the lack of individuals from historically excluded populations in the STEM fields (Bybee, 2013). Standardized test scores remain a focus, yet policy expectations for what and how to teach maintain traditional pedagogy. In the United States, since the 1970s, there has been great attention paid to providing access to STEM disciplines and increasing a sense of belonging in STEM. This was an important step forward, of course, but continuing to use comparative terms such as *underrepresented* and *historically excluded* perpetuates and promotes the notion that there is an accepted norm against which to measure. In the United States, this norm has usually

Figure 1.1

A Scholar Engages in an Integrated STEM Learning Experience

Source: Julie Sicks-Panus.

been (and often continues to be) whiteness-centered, male, cis-gendered, ableist, heteronormative, and Eurocentric. In fact, those who are often described by policymakers and others in the United States as "underrepresented" or "historically excluded" are actually part of the global majority. The term *global majority* is a term that has emerged in recent years to describe the world's population, which is predominantly nonwhite, non-Western, and non-European. Likewise, *people of the global majority* (PGM) is a term that encourages those of African, Arab, Asian, and Latin American descent to recognize that together they make up close to 80% of people in the world (Maharaj & Campbell-Stephens, 2021). *Global majority* in this sense, then, includes, but is not limited to, people of color, women, members of the LGBTQIA+ community, people with disabilities, people whose incomes are below the federal poverty threshold, indigenous people, and other historically marginalized groups. The term *global majority* is meant to highlight the importance of acknowledging and respecting the experiences and perspectives of people from all corners of the globe and to challenge the idea that Western culture and values are universal. We encourage a discussion of the term *global majority* and how conversations in your setting can be recentered with additional perspectives.

Stop, Think, Reflect (1B)

1. What will you need to consider to ensure all your scholars have access to high-quality STEM learning experiences? (Reflect on instructional supports, access to materials, language supports, etc.)

2. What classroom norms will you establish to ensure all scholars feel safe?

3. What does it look like to cultivate a sense of belonging in STEM in your classroom?

4. What positive outcomes can occur when we work with people from different backgrounds?

5. How can we leverage scholars' varied backgrounds in a STEM learning environment?

 Available for download at **qrs.ly/s9f1lux**

Our aim in this conversation about the STEM status quo is to raise awareness and, more important, address direct actions we can take as educators to create a more inclusive environment. Becoming STEM system disruptors requires recognizing and challenging the norms and practices that have been historically exclusive and promoting inclusive and equitable approaches that value, cultivate, and include diverse perspectives and experiences. As educators, we need to connect to our scholars' lived experiences and bring them into the STEM conversation. When we do this, our scholars feel safe, valued, and empowered to do STEM.

Becoming STEM System Disruptors: An Equity-Oriented, Culturally Responsive Approach

To disrupt the STEM status quo, every scholar must have access to high-quality integrated STEM learning opportunities, but access alone is not enough. It is also necessary to focus intentionally on equity to counteract the deeply rooted traditions in STEM education, which have privileged a few and marginalized many. When we refer to privilege within the context of STEM communities, we are referring to having certain advantages or benefits that provide persons with a head start or easier access to opportunities within the STEM fields. This can range from having a financially stable background, to being a part of a demographic group that is traditionally overrepresented in STEM fields, to having access to influential networks or connections. When we refer to marginalized within the context of STEM communities, we are referring to individuals or groups that typically face barriers, discrimination, and/or limited access to opportunities within the STEM fields (Aish et al., 2018). This can be based on a number of factors, including, but not limited to, geography, race, gender, ethnicity, ableness, financial stability, and other forms of social identity. Further, persons from marginalized communities often encounter more obstacles than those who are not, especially around representation, access to resources, inclusion, educational opportunities, and equitable treatment. Recognizing and talking about privilege and marginalization within the STEM community is important because it can help to directly disrupt the STEM status quo, address systemic inequities, and create pathways to more inclusive environments. By addressing and having conversations, we recognize that not everyone starts with the same advantages and thus we can begin to disrupt the systems that have continued to oppress marginalized populations. Together, and through the work in this book, we can become STEM system disruptors by leveling the playing field and ensuring equitable opportunities for individuals from all backgrounds to thrive in STEM and their communities.

Our work is guided by the Equity-Oriented STEM Literacy Framework (Jackson et al., 2021; Figure 1.2), which goes "beyond platitudes of 'diversity, equity, and inclusion' and the traditional focus on access by illuminating the complexities of disrupting the status quo and rightfully transforming integrated STEM education in ways that provide equitable opportunities and access to all learners" (p. 5). See Figure 1.2.

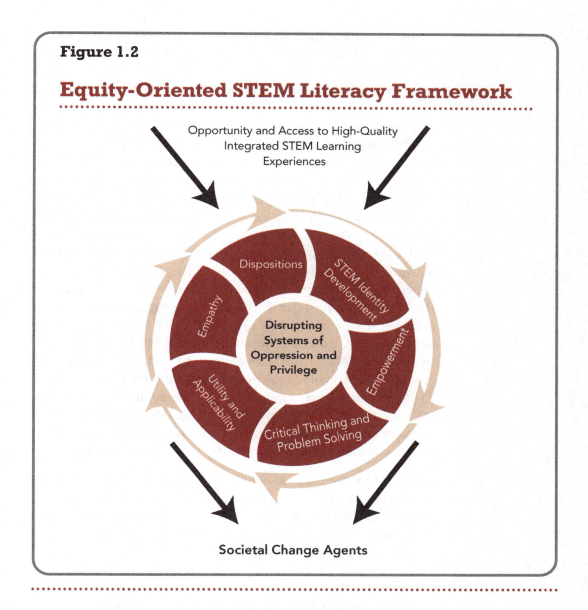

Figure 1.2

Equity-Oriented STEM Literacy Framework

Opportunity and Access to High-Quality Integrated STEM Learning Experiences

Dispositions

STEM Identity Development

Empathy

Disrupting Systems of Oppression and Privilege

Empowerment

Utility and Applicability

Critical Thinking and Problem Solving

Societal Change Agents

Having access to high-quality STEM learning experiences fosters the **development of STEM identity** whereby all scholars begin to view themselves as STEM learners, doers, and thinkers as they engage in **critical thinking to seek solutions.** We have all been asked, "When am I ever going to use this?" More times than not, we have responded, "You need to know this because it is important for you to know," or "To be successful in the next subject," or "Just because." By engaging scholars in high-quality STEM learning experiences, they see the **utility and applicability** of the STEM disciplines and the concepts and material they are learning. Thus, scholars are positioned to understand the *why* of their learning, why this is important, why it is relevant to their lives, and why knowing this information is empowering. Within high-quality integrated STEM learning experiences—think about examples such as designing a prosthetic leg for another scholar in need or designing a structure to combat a food desert in a local community—scholars develop **empathy**. Empathy embodies equity as it builds scholars' interest, ensures relevance and meaning to STEM, and empowers scholars as someone who can be part of the solution. Approaching STEM from an empathetic lens also provides more equitable solutions to our communities and the world. Historically, empathy has typically not been strongly associated with STEM or STEM learning experiences. We intentionally incorporate empathy as one of the components because empathy fosters humanization and care within STEM. It makes the STEM learning experience more meaningful to scholars and provides the passion and purpose (Bush & Cook, 2019; Bush et al., 2022).). Empathy illuminates the utility and applicability of the STEM learning experience. Through high-quality integrated STEM learning experiences, scholars develop productive STEM **dispositions** whereby they become interested in and have a positive attitude toward learning STEM. In this way, all scholars are **empowered** to ask questions, solve challenges, and be societal change agents in the world in which they live.

As educators, we have an obligation to ensure every scholar, and specifically every person from the global majority, has a sense of belonging in STEM (Jackson et al., 2021). However, white, Eurocentric norms often maintain the STEM status quo, in many ways, including, but not limited to

- An emphasis on individual achievement and competition, rather than collaboration and community building

- Hierarchical, authoritarian, and similar power structures, where those in positions of power are less likely to listen to and incorporate perspectives of those in positions of less power

- Focus on objectivity and neutrality, which can ignore the influence of cultural biases and assumptions in research and decision-making

To become STEM system disruptors, the education community has used the approach known as culturally responsive teaching. Culturally responsive teaching uses "the cultural knowledge, prior experiences, frames of reference, and performance styles of ethnically diverse students to make learning encounters more relevant to and effective for them" (Gay, 2018, p. 36). This approach acknowledges that scholars from different cultural backgrounds may have unique ways of learning, communicating, and understanding the world, and it seeks to create a learning environment that values, elevates, and sees these differences as strengths. Adopting this approach provides scholars with opportunities to learn more about their own cultures as well as the cultures of their classmates. We contend this empowers scholars to become global thinkers who are passionate and knowledgeable and therefore able to solve challenges to make the world better, help their communities thrive, create a better life for themselves and others, and compassionately analyze situations from multiple perspectives. This also cultivates a way of being that is empathy-centric and altruistic. Culturally responsive teaching challenges the standardization driven by the dominant cultural norms. Table 1.1 provides common characteristics of the STEM status quo, why it's harmful in the STEM contexts, and how it is addressed in this book. Throughout this book, you will see explicit and intentional focus on culturally responsive teaching practices that move to disrupt the STEM status quo.

Table 1.1

Be on the Lookout: STEM Status Quo Characteristics

STEM STATUS QUO CHARACTERISTICS	WHY IT'S HARMFUL IN STEM	HOW WE ADDRESSED IT IN THIS BOOK
Perfectionism	In STEM, we tend to focus on right or wrong and the final solution rather than the progress, and the mistakes that move us toward progress. When we focus on being perfect, or getting it right the first time, we lose out on the learning opportunities. Further, it causes additional anxieties that often build upon each other through subsequent learning experiences. While we can certainly strive for excellence, excellence can be a messy winding road, which is not equivalent to perfection.	We address process, multiple iterations, embracing mistakes, and productive struggle. The chapter-opening stories provide examples of building a culture within the learning experience that embraces messiness, pivots, and an openness to share and learn new things by all participants, including the educator.

(Continued)

STEM STATUS QUO CHARACTERISTICS	WHY IT'S HARMFUL IN STEM	HOW WE ADDRESSED IT IN THIS BOOK
Objectivity	In STEM, there is often the belief that you have to be objective or stay "neutral," especially as it relates to emotions. It can often show up when you are asked to make a "logical" decision, which often means linear decision-making without regard or thoughts of others.	We emphasize and encourage empathy in solution seeking. Empathy is often how our scholars connect with each other—within and outside their lived experiences. Listening, getting feedback, and researching the impact of an idea or solution on others helps to take in all perspectives and voices.
One Right Way	In STEM, most often in mathematics, there is often the belief or underlying notion that there is only one right way or a preferred way to complete something. When someone doesn't do it the same way as others, the others assume the other way is the wrong way.	We share examples and stories that embrace scholars' sharing multiple solutions and ideas. The rubrics make explicit that the expectation is multiple iterations of trials. We are more focused on the process rather than the final solution.
Paternalism	In STEM, this shows up as someone who holds a position of power and controls the decision-making and defines rules, criteria, policy, and so on. This shows up in education, especially when scholars know they do not have the power and are marginalized from decision-making processes.	It is easy to think that in education, a teacher is always going to be paternalistic. However, we point out direct ways to give choice to scholars, elevate their voices, and provide open spaces for them to give input in deciding success criteria.
Qualified	In STEM, when we talk of someone being "qualified," the criteria are not always consistent or clear, and the notions can be based on antiquated definitions of success (e.g., the one speaking the loudest must be confident and thus correct; the one who is the first to take credit must be the one who knows the most). We also might incorrectly think that only adults with specialized degrees and skills can contribute solutions to authentic STEM obstacles.	We present inclusionary language when sharing stories and positioning scholars within the suggested learning experience. Within the learning experiences, the scholars are the experts. They are the ones carrying out the practices, producing the various solutions or ideas, and communicating them to the various stakeholders. The only qualification a scholar needs in your classroom or setting is to be present, in whatever way that looks for them.

STEM STATUS QUO CHARACTERISTICS	WHY IT'S HARMFUL IN STEM	HOW WE ADDRESSED IT IN THIS BOOK
Either/Or and the Binary	In STEM, this positions ideas, solutions, options, issues, and so on as yes or no; either/or; right or wrong; for or against; and so forth. In STEM especially, this type of thinking tends to oversimplify, in a negative way, the complex tasks or experiences our scholars often face in their life.	We encourage the use of multiple options (beyond two) and an openness to what these options or scenarios look like.
Progress Is Bigger/ More and Quantity Over Quality	In life and in STEM, we live in a more is better, bigger is better society. However, sometimes solutions in STEM involve taking away factors, simplifying processes, and taking less actions rather than more. In other words, subtracting can also be a solution, not just adding. Sometimes more people, materials, or money are associated with progress, but this isn't always the case.	We include a focused emphasis on progress being more about the quality of the product, idea, or trial. Further, there is less emphasis on doing something repeatedly over and over again until you achieve "memorization" or "retainment." Rather, we focus on meaningful interactions with the content that will help to forge a connection between the scholar, the content, and the experience.
Defensiveness	In STEM, this usually shows up in the response to feedback to an idea, solution, scenario, and so on. Instead of thinking and taking in the feedback, we are prone to get defensive and start forming our defensive answers in our head, thus taking away the ability to listen and reflect. Further, when defensiveness shows up, it will often shut down those who are participating as it makes it difficult to raise new ideas, and thus those who are met with defensiveness may be afraid to speak their ideas or truth.	We include various ways scholars' voices are and can be elevated, especially in giving feedback. We also include strategies for how feedback can be received in a more useful way.
Power Hoarding	In STEM, this is most often seen in collaborative settings, or settings where multiple people engage with one another. It is harmful in that someone tries to exert their power or control into or over a situation. Many times, they see themselves as doing what's "best" for the group and others.	We share stories about collaborative experiences where scholars are working together and sharing ideas. In the examples and diving deeper, there is a continued focus on collaboration. In real-world contexts, collaboration is a key component within the community or workplace. Creating shared, positive, collaborative experiences with scholars can help define and provide examples to scholars of how groups can function together toward their main goal or focus.

(Continued)

STEM STATUS QUO CHARACTERISTICS	WHY IT'S HARMFUL IN STEM	HOW WE ADDRESSED IT IN THIS BOOK
Urgency	In STEM, this shows up often in timelines and deadlines. How fast can we get something finished, even if it's poor quality. Further, timed tests or events create a sense of urgency that is unreasonable and unrealistic in real-world contexts.	We emphasize the practices as processes that don't necessarily have an end point. Or if there is an end point, it can look different for different groups of scholars. When addressing urgency, it's important to underscore setting realistic expectations and including scholars in the conversation about realistic expectations. This not only helps to elevate their voices and disrupt the STEM status quo characteristic—paternalism—but also helps them to have ownership in creating a realistic timeline or expectations to complete within a given time period.

Source: Adapted in part from the ideas in Okun (2021); Hawthorne (2022). See these for more examples and antidotes.

By explicitly addressing and challenging the STEM status quo, especially as educators, we are challenging our own power dynamics, listening to and valuing diverse perspectives, educating ourselves, and, most important, holding ourselves accountable. Regardless of our own racial identity, gender, social class, abilities, and other personal identifying factors, it is important to recognize and understand our own privilege so that we can all be STEM system disruptors and work toward a more equitable and inclusive society.

Integrated STEM Practices Unpacked

You are likely familiar with the Standards for Mathematical Practices (SMPs), Science and Engineering Practices (SEPs), and the Technology and Engineering Practices (TEPs). Table 1.2 identifies each practice for mathematics, science, and technology and engineering and the things to look for regarding scholar engagement and outcomes within each practice.

Table 1.2

Science and Engineering, Technology and Engineering, and Mathematics Practices

PRACTICE STANDARD	STANDARD	WHEN ENGAGING IN THE STANDARD, SCHOLARS SHOULD:
Science and Engineering Practices (Next Generation Science Standards [NGSS Lead States], 2013)	1. Ask questions (science) and define problems (engineering)	Start the first steps of the scientific inquiry process and engineering design process by asking questions and defining problems.
	2. Develop and use models	Construct models to represent explanations and ideas.
	3. Plan and carry out investigations	Investigate and observe the world using a systematic process to determine questions that need to be expired or problems that need to be solved.
	4. Analyze and interpret data	Use data to look for patterns and structures that can be used to make design decisions or inform investigations.
	5. Use mathematics and computational thinking	Use mathematics to represent data and find solutions to problems.
	6. Construct explanations and design solutions	Find the outcomes of science (explanations) and engineering (solutions).
	7. Engage in arguments from evidence	Engage in the process used to find explanations and solutions to problems.
	8. Obtain, evaluate, and communicate information	Engage in meaningful discourse and dialogue.
Technology and Engineering Practices (International Technology and Engineering Educators Association [ITEEA], 2020)	1. Systems thinking	Recognize how technologies are interconnected.
	2. Creativity	Use innovative thinking and skills to solve problems.
	3. Making and doing	Design and build products and systems.
	4. Critical thinking	Engage in reasoning to make informed decisions.
	5. Optimism	Improve the world around you and view that in every challenge, there are opportunities.
	6. Collaboration	Work as part of a team to find solutions to problems.
	7. Communication	A tool to understand the needs of others and a process used to engage in problem solving.
	8. Attention to ethics	Focus on the impact decisions make on the world around them.

(Continued)

PRACTICE STANDARD	STANDARD	WHEN ENGAGING IN THE STANDARD, SCHOLARS SHOULD:
Standard for Mathematical Practice (National Governors Association Center for Best Practices & Council of Chief State School Officers, 2010)	1. Make sense of problems and persevere in solving them	Make sense of problems and engage in sustained problem-solving experiences.
	2. Reason abstractly and quantitatively	Contextualize and decontextualize problems.
	3. Construct viable arguments and critique the reasonings of others	Engage in meaningful mathematical discourse and dialogue.
	4. Model with mathematics	Use mathematics to solve problems in everyday life, society, and the workplace.
	5. Use appropriate tools strategically	Know and use appropriate mathematical tools.
	6. Attend to precision	Communicate mathematical understanding clearly using different representations.
	7. Look for and make use of structure	Find patterns that can be applied to new situations.
	8. Look for and express regularity in repeated reasoning	Recognize and make sense of patterns.

Each of these existing practice standards focuses on problem solving. In science, scholars solve problems as they engage in the scientific inquiry process. They formulate hypotheses, design and conduct experiments, and interpret the results. The SEPs are designed to increase scholars' curiosity, interest, and motivation as they develop proficiency in understanding how to investigate problems and explain phenomena occurring in the world (National Research Council, 2012). In the mathematics SMPs, scholars make conjectures, justify conclusions, represent solutions, and evaluate the reasonableness of their results when solving problems. In the technology and engineering practices, scholars design and create solutions to improve existing technology and better the world around them as they engage in the engineering design process. While all three sets of practices (i.e., SMPs, SEPs, and TEPs) engage scholars in problem solving in their respective disciplines, solution seeking of challenges (small and large) in our community and society necessitates a more holistic and flexible approach (Roberts et al., 2022).

The focus of this book is on solution seeking through integrating the practices of the STEM disciplines in ways that create impactful STEM learning experiences that position all scholars as STEM thinkers and doers. We identify these practices as the Integrated STEM Practices (ISPs). We synthesized the Standards for Mathematical Practices, Science and Engineering Practices, and the Technology and Engineering Practices to develop the ISPs. The ISPs are grounded in the Equity-Oriented STEM Literacy Framework (see Figure 1.2) and culturally responsive STEM pedagogy. The four ISPs are

1. use critical and creative thinking to seek solutions,

2. collaborate and use appropriate tools to engage in iterative design,

3. communicate solutions based on evidence and data, and

4. recognize and use structures in real-world systems (see Figure 1.3).

ISP 1: USE CRITICAL AND CREATIVE THINKING TO SEEK SOLUTIONS

Scholars use creativity and critical thinking to explore and solve nonroutine, real-world challenges (Henriksen, 2014). Scholars persevere and actively use models as they work toward understanding and seeking a solution to a particular challenge. As scholars seek solutions, they work to understand the challenge and have the fortitude to continue when they encounter difficulties or obstacles along their journey toward finding a solution (SMP 1, SEP 1, TEP 5). They persist. They engage in scientific inquiry by asking questions to critically reason and make sense of the challenge (SEP 1, TEP 4). As scholars creatively work (TEP 2) toward their solution(s), they use models (SMP 4), and mathematics and computational thinking (SEP 5). As the scholars critically and creatively think, they also use reasoning to make informed decisions toward their solution (TEP 4). By engaging in these practices, scholars ultimately view the challenges they encounter as opportunities to improve their world (TEP 5).

ISP 2: COLLABORATE AND USE APPROPRIATE TOOLS TO ENGAGE IN ITERATIVE DESIGN

Scholars collaborate to use appropriate tools to plan, test, and refine their solutions to nonroutine, real-world problems. Collaboration (TEP 6) is essential when solving challenges. We learn from one another. As scholars plan and carry out investigations (SEP 3) using a systematic process, they strategically draw upon appropriate tools to use (SMP 5). They are fully invested in the process

Figure 1.3

How the ISPs Are Situated Within SMPs, SEPs, and TEPs

Technology & Engineering Practices (ITEEA, 2020)	Science & Engineering Practices (NGSS, 2013)	Standards for Mathematical Practice (CCSSO, 2010)	Integrated STEM Practices (Roberts et al., 2022)
2. Creativity 4. Critical Thinking 5. Optimism	1. Asking questions and defining problems 5. Using mathematics and computational thinking.	1. Make sense of problems and persevere in solving them 4. Model with mathematics	Use critical and creative thinking to seek solutions
3. Making & Doing 6. Collaboration	3. Planning and carrying out investigations	2. Reason abstractly and quantitatively 4. Model with mathematics 5. Use appropriate tools strategically 6. Attend to precision	Collaborate and use appropriate tools to engage in iterative design
7. Communication	4. Analyzing and interpreting data 5. Using mathematics and computational thinking 6. Constructing explanations and designing solutions 7. Engaging in arguments from evidence 8. Obtaining, evaluating, and communicating	3. Construct viable arguments and critique the reasoning of others 4. Model with mathematics	Communicate solutions based on evidence and data
1. Systems Thinking 8. Attention to Ethics	2. Developing and using models	4. Model with mathematics 7. Look for and make use of structure 8. Look for and express regularity in repeated reasoning	Recognize and use structures in real-world systems

of making and doing (TEP 3) and are intentional on refining their model (SMP 4). They showcase their knowledge through reasoning abstractly and quantitatively. When they do this, they attend to precision (SMP 6) and continue their collaboration (TEP 6) with one another.

ISP 3: COMMUNICATE SOLUTIONS BASED ON EVIDENCE AND DATA

Scholars communicate to gather information needed to solve a challenge, share ideas and strategies to create a plan, and share solutions using effective presentations. Communication is an essential skill for scholars. Scholars actively listen to others (TEP 7) and look for patterns and structures that can be used to make design decisions or inform investigations (SMP 4, SEP 4, SEP 6). They articulate, justify, and critique their and others' reasoning (SMP 3, SEP 4, SEP 8) using evidence (SEP 7).

ISP 4: RECOGNIZE AND USE STRUCTURES IN REAL-WORLD SYSTEMS

Scholars look for structures within and across content areas to apply known ideas to new real-world situations and evaluate the reasonableness of their proposed solutions within the context of the system. Scholars apply structures within and across disciplines to solve challenges within today's society (SMP 8). To do so, scholars develop models to represent systems and test their solutions for success and failures (SEP 2). The world is interconnected. Scholars work toward finding solutions to challenges focused on the entire system (TEP 1). They look for patterns (SMP 7) and use these patterns to help determine the reasonableness of their solutions (SMP 4). Scholars care about the world and consider the impact their solutions have on the world (TEP 8).

The ISPs are not designed to replace the important disciplinary learning that occurs in mathematics and science classrooms. Instead, the ISPs focus on practices scholars exhibit that are important to STEM as an integrated discipline where they apply disciplinary content knowledge to seek solutions to authentic challenges. These practices will be evident in performance tasks where mathematics and science teachers collaborate, in technology and engineering projects, in STEM classrooms, and in informal STEM learning settings. In all of these settings, the specific content addressed can change, but a constant is scholars' use of the ISPs.

••• SO YOU'VE BEEN TOLD . . .

REALITY CHECK!

Throughout the book you will find informative boxes that contain "So You've Been Told" statements and "Reality Check" responses from our team. These boxes will combat misconceptions and help you reframe your approaches to integrated STEM teaching. You'll usually find them sprinkled throughout each chapter throughout the rest of the book, but here we've presented several for you to consider at this point in our discussion.

••• SO YOU'VE BEEN TOLD . . .

STEM tasks take too much time and include too many components.

REALITY CHECK!

Meaningful STEM tasks can be small yet mighty! The context can stem (pun intended!) from a single curiosity from a scholar, something they have noticed outside, at school, in their community, or a wondering from a current event. Sure, you can implement large-scale, long-term STEM tasks, but it doesn't have to be of that magnitude. STEM tasks are only as big as you make them. We suggest first doing what you can with the time you have and let the excitement spread throughout your classroom and school. Reaching out to your colleagues could be beneficial. It is very possible that others in your building (or network outside of your building) have some great ideas that could complement your task or spark your imagination for a new task. They may even want to help and work on it with you! These conversations will build buy-in as you work to advocate for more support and time for integrated STEM! ●

••• SO YOU'VE BEEN TOLD . . .

There is no time—we are already rushed to teach mathematics and science; there is no time for integrated STEM.

REALITY CHECK!

Integrated STEM IS Mathematics and IS Science. STEM is a pathway to working smarter, not harder. STEM learning experiences grounded in the ISPs help you to engage your scholars in the STEM disciplines simultaneously. In other words, it's not adding to your plate; it's instead a more meaningful approach that saves time in the long run. A teacher who implemented an integrated STEM unit in her second-grade classroom exclaimed,

"We definitely don't talk a lot about angles going into like what are the specific angles, 90 [degrees] and 180 [degrees]. And they know that there are angles to shapes, but we don't talk about what they are. They actually learned a lot about angles and enjoyed that, with the launcher and putting all that together. So I thought a lot of our math ideas were ones that the kids kind of picked up on it on their own. It wasn't something that we had taught yet. So that was cool to see. Because we hadn't done shapes, we haven't done measurement. And so it was like a quick, 'Okay, when we go to measure our shadows, this is what you're going to do.' And then they had to automatically go and do it, but they were doing something real world. So they had actually picked up on it very quickly as opposed to just measuring something on their paper. So I thought that was cool that they were learning some of those skills, just by doing it and trying it, but not really with my telling them, this is exactly how you do it. They went and tried it and learned it."

The key is intentionally drawing out scholars' learning through the STEM tasks you implement, the probing questions you ask, and the authentic assessments you plan. We are working smarter and not harder. You'll learn more about how to do this throughout the book. ●

●●● SO YOU'VE BEEN TOLD . . .

Not all students can do STEM.

REALITY CHECK!

All scholars should be empowered and given the agency to be STEM thinkers, tinkers, and doers. As educators, we must provide opportunity and access to high-quality integrated STEM learning experiences. To ensure integrated STEM actively positions every scholar as a valuable member of the STEM community, we draw upon the *Equity-Oriented STEM Literacy Framework* (Jackson et al., 2021). The model disrupts the STEM status quo by providing opportunity and access for scholars to participate in high-quality learning experiences. For the scholars who typically think they cannot do STEM, they see the rationale for their learning experience through the utility and applicability of STEM through their engagement of the ISPs. We know you will be astonished with what your scholars can do as they engage in the ISPs. ●

Jumpstarting Your Work: Integrated STEM Educator Check-in Tool

We'd like to invite you to now jumpstart your journey! We provide an Integrated STEM Educator Check-in Tool (available in the online implementation toolkit) as a "pulse check" to use throughout your integrated STEM journey. This tool holistically embodies our Equity-Oriented STEM Literacy Framework and focuses on your current thoughts and open-ended prompts that can be used in whole or part to obtain feedback, gain deeper insights, or plan. This tool is not a formal survey instrument and is not intended to be used as an evaluation tool; rather, it is meant to be used as a tool to gauge starting points and growth. Figure 1.4 is a snapshot of the Integrated STEM Educator Check-in Tool.

Figure 1.4

Snapshot of the Integrated STEM Educator Check-in Tool

	BELIEFS	
1	I believe integrated STEM learning experiences have great value.	1 2 3 4 5
2	I believe scholars can play a key role in leading their own learning regarding integrated STEM while the teacher acts as a facilitator.	1 2 3 4 5
3	I believe integrated STEM learning experiences are a place where I can draw and leverage the strengths of each scholar.	1 2 3 4 5
4	I believe integrated STEM learning experiences increase scholars' interest in STEM careers.	1 2 3 4 5
5	I believe integrated STEM learning is critical to the development of the next generation of thinkers, advocates, and creators.	1 2 3 4 5

 Available for download at **qrs.ly/s9f1lux**

We provide access to the full tool in the online implementation toolkit. We envision the Integrated STEM Educator Check-in Tool could be used

- as a self-check of your own personal growth as you read this book;
- if you are embarking on this journey as part of school or district initiative, every educator involved (including administration and paraprofessionals) could use the check-in at the beginning of the journey and every few months to gauge individual and collective shifts in thinking and implementation;
- as a pre, midpoint, and post check-in to gauge shifts in thinking and implementation from a long-term sustained professional development initiative;
- as a pre, midpoint, and post check-in for an integrated STEM education course for preservice or in-service teachers and coaches; and
- in many other ways.

In each chapter, we provide a collection of discussion questions that can be used to reflect and ponder on the ideas discussed within the chapter. The questions could also be used as book study prompts to spark rich discussion with your team!

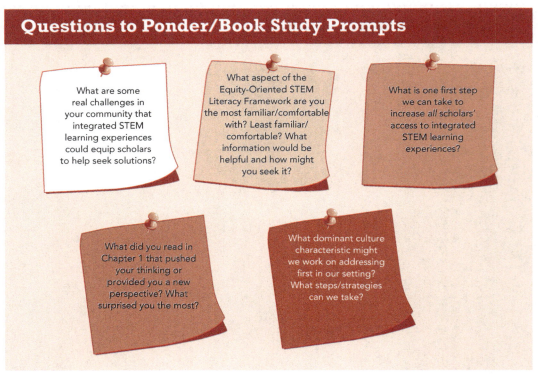

Questions to Ponder/Book Study Prompts

What are some real challenges in your community that integrated STEM learning experiences could equip scholars to help seek solutions?

What aspect of the Equity-Oriented STEM Literacy Framework are you the most familiar/comfortable with? Least familiar/comfortable? What information would be helpful and how might you seek it?

What is one first step we can take to increase *all* scholars' access to integrated STEM learning experiences?

What did you read in Chapter 1 that pushed your thinking or provided you a new perspective? What surprised you the most?

What dominant culture characteristic might we work on addressing first in our setting? What steps/strategies can we take?

 Available for download at **qrs.ly/s9f1lux**

Organization of This Book

Although multiple high-quality STEM learning experiences are featured throughout the book, the purpose is not to focus on the specific STEM content. Instead, we provide very tangible examples of the ISPs in action! Content will shine through indirectly as we share stories of each ISP. Similar to the Standards for Mathematical Practices (SMPs), Science and Engineering Practices (SEPs), and the Technology and Engineering Practices (TEPs), the ISPs are relevant for scholars in grades PreK–12. We offer both an elementary (PreK–5) volume and a secondary (6–12) volume of the book to exemplify what the ISPs look like, sound like, and feel like at the elementary and secondary levels. To recap, in this chapter, we shared our core beliefs about integrated STEM learning, introduced you to the Equity-Oriented STEM Literacy Framework, and provided an overview of the ISPs. Now you might be wondering, what do high-quality STEM learning experiences look like, sound like, and feel like in the classroom? Throughout this book, we draw upon and highlight high-quality STEM learning experiences to describe the ISPs and their importance within the STEM learning experience. We encourage you to visit our online implementation toolkit as you journey through this book. It contains helpful resources you can adapt, adopt, and use along the way!

Planning, implementation, and assessment of impactful STEM learning experiences leveraging the ISPs warrants a nontraditional approach to "lesson planning." In Chapters 2 to 5, we take a deep dive into each of the four ISPs. In each of these chapters, we provide real-life examples of STEM learning experiences focused on a specific ISP. We recognize that scholars' lived experiences vary, and so what is real life to one may not be real life to another. We encourage you to consider how to connect the ideas and contexts to all scholars. This could be through videos, pictures, researching a topic, and so on. In this book, you will be able to visualize the ISP in action. Our goal is to help you translate this visualization to your scholars and their learning experiences. Importantly, these chapters will leave you with a strong understanding of the innovative, deep, and impactful contributions of scholars when their strengths are leveraged (see Kobett & Karp, 2020) and they are positioned as belonging in STEM. Throughout the chapters, we will highlight the connections between the ISP and the Equity-Oriented STEM Literacy Framework. We include in each of these chapters helpful resources to guide your work, both in the book and in the online implementation toolkit. We unpack common misconceptions about STEM instruction within each ISP. We also intentionally focus on assessing scholars' STEM learning in authentic ways. We provide additional examples and resources that showcase how scholars might develop their abilities within each ISP. After reading Chapters 2 to 5, you will have a strong understanding of each of the four ISPs; have a firm grasp of the key components of planning, implementing, and assessing meaningful high-quality STEM learning experiences; and begin to see how the ISPs are actually quite intertwined.

Chapter 6 focuses on reimagining STEM tasks. We consider the characteristics of high-quality STEM tasks and how they embody the ISPs. We provide examples and resources that showcase how scholars might develop their abilities across multiple ISPs simultaneously. We include a roadmap and conversation starters that will walk you through the planning, implementation, and assessment of an ISP learning experience. Importantly, we ground this work in the components of the Equity-Oriented STEM Literacy Framework. In Chapter 6, you'll have an opportunity to complete the STEM planning tool, try out some of the resources, and plan for how you will assess learning. In Chapter 7, we explore the heart and spirit of the ISPs and Equity-Oriented STEM Literacy Framework. We discuss shifting away from a checklist approach to an ISP mindset and why it's up to us as educators to embark on this work. Finally, we leave you with a sense of collective action! Share your thoughts to our online sharing space using the hashtag #STEMISPs.

ISP 1: USE CRITICAL AND CREATIVE THINKING TO SEEK SOLUTIONS

In the following story, you will meet Mrs. Lee, a second-grade teacher who engages her scholars in the ISP of using critical and creative thinking to seek solutions. As you read, look for . . .

- Ways Mrs. Lee facilitates critical and creative thinking

- How scholars use critical and creative thinking to seek solutions

- Ways the learning experience provides opportunities for scholars to engage in ISP 1

●●● THE STORY OF MRS. LEE

Mrs. Lee (she/her) hurriedly checked to make sure she had a variety of small screwdrivers, paper bowls, and a range of batteries before her scholars began entering her classroom. Mrs. Lee, a second-grade teacher, was nervous because she had not implemented a STEM task before. She was excited to try and thought her scholars would get engaged in the STEM Task: Deconstructing and Reconstructing an Object.

As her scholars began entering the classroom, Mrs. Lee noticed they were excitedly sharing the nonfunctioning items they brought with them. Mrs. Lee had several nonfunctioning items scholars could use if they wished (i.e., calculators, spring scales, wall clocks, old nonworking laptops), and some scholars brought their own object from home.

Kiara had a small black analog clock. "This has been stuck at 4:15 for the last 3 weeks," Kiara told Mekhi.

"Oh, that's definitely not working. I have this calculator. The numbers don't show up when I turn it on," Mekhi shared.

"It's kinda weird that we had to bring in stuff that doesn't work. What are we going to do with all of this broken stuff?" Kiara wondered aloud.

"Please get out a pencil and the item you brought with you today," Mrs. Lee announced. While scholars were getting pencils and their items, Mrs. Lee handed out a structured reflection tool designed to help her scholars document their learning throughout the STEM task.

STEM Structured Reflection Tool

Deconstructing and Reconstructing an Object

What you need...

- Item or toy that no longer works (preferably with moving parts and possibly a motor)
- Tools to take it apart
- A bowl or bag to keep parts
- Device with camera (optional)

1. Record how your object works when functioning properly. (Written, oral, or video blog)

   Does it move something?

   Does it make noise?

   Be as specific as possible.

2. What is not working on your object?

   Which part that you identified previously does not work?

   If it is not in your previous list, then possibly you need to add it.

   Is the problem visible?

"With your shoulder partner, I want you to take turns talking about the item you brought with you today. Explain what the item is, how it functions, if it is supposed to move or make noise. Be as specific as possible. Once each person has shared, write one sentence explaining what your object is and one sentence explaining how it should work. You have 8 minutes to complete this step. What questions do you have?" Mrs. Lee told the scholars to begin, set the timer for 8 minutes, and started circulating to listen to scholars' conversations and probe their thinking.

"I'll go first," Mekhi said. "So this was my brother's calculator. When I turn it on the numbers don't show up on the screen. It's not supposed to make any sounds but it is supposed to show the numbers."

"OK my turn," Kiara said. "This is a clock. It's supposed to work like a normal clock does but the hands are stuck at 4:15. It's not an alarm clock, so it doesn't really make sounds," Kiara explained.

"Does it make those ticking noises like some clocks do?" Mekhi asked.

"Oh yeah! It used to when it was working. I didn't even think about that as a sound," Kiara replied. "We better write all of this down on our papers."

After the scholars shared, Mrs. Lee showed them a 3D pen that had stopped working last week. "This 3D pen extrudes filament (plastic) that can be used to create cool objects! It has to be plugged in to work. The pen heats up an extruder so that it melts the filament. This small button triggers a motor that pushes filament through the extruder. There is also a slider that changes the speed of the motor." Noticing several scholars adding more to their descriptions after hearing her describe the 3D pen, Mrs. Lee gave everyone an opportunity to revise their description.

"Now, I want you to think about how you would describe what's wrong with your object and describe some possible solutions. For example, with this 3D pen, filament goes in but it doesn't come out the extruder. Work with your shoulder partner to explain which part doesn't work, if the problem is visible, and brainstorm some solutions. Be sure to write down at least one idea you talked about," Mrs. Lee said.

Kiara looked at Mekhi. "The hands aren't moving on my clock. That's visible."

"How would you try to fix that?" Mekhi asked.

"Hmmm. I'm not sure. I've tried replacing the batteries and that didn't work. Maybe there's more to it than just batteries not working," Kiara stated.

"Maybe you'll have to take it apart and see if there's something else going on since changing the batteries didn't work. The problem with mine is that the numbers don't show up. It looks like everything is fine. But you can see that it doesn't show anything when you push the buttons."

"So how could you fix that?" Kiara inquired.

"Maybe I'll have to take it apart and see if a piece inside is broken." After the conversation, Kiara and Mekhi wrote their ideas down on their structured reflection tool.

Next, Mrs. Lee said, "Now that you have brainstormed problems and solutions, I want you to decide if you need to break down your object and, if so, how. Are there any screws holding the item together? Are there other parts? What tools will you need? Once you decide what tools you need, you can meet me at the back table to collect your materials. Remember our conversation about safely using the tools and watching for sharp edges. Please wear protective eyeglasses as you work. As you break your object down, use your structured reflection tool to document the steps you take. You can also take pictures to help you remember where parts go. Sketching is important to illustrate the object, the changes you are making, and your thinking! As you take apart your object, be sure to place parts in a bowl so you don't lose anything."

The scholars excitedly worked to collect their tools and break down their objects. After 10 minutes of work time, Mrs. Lee pushed them toward the next part. "Once you have broken down your object, reexamine your solution.

- Do you think it will work?

- Is there a different problem than what you hypothesized?

- Will you need a new solution?

- Keep coming back to this step if your solution doesn't work."

Mrs. Lee walked around the room observing scholars, asking them questions, and offering suggestions and encouragement if they became frustrated. At Kiara and Mekhi's table, Mrs. Lee noticed a puzzled look on Mekhi's face.

"Mekhi, what do you think will make your calculator display work again?" Mrs. Lee asked.

"I'm not really sure. I've looked at everything and can't find anything wrong. The wires are all connected. Nothing looks broken. It just isn't working!" Mekhi explained. (See Figure 2.1.)

Figure 2.1

Mekhi Deconstructs a Calculator to Examine Why It Doesn't Work

Source: Tracy Young

"Do you know what this is?" Mrs. Lee inquired while pointing to the circular silver battery. Mekhi shook his head. "This is a special kind of battery," Mrs. Lee explained. "I have some at the materials table." Mekhi quickly got up to go get a new battery.

"Kiara, tell me where you are with fixing your clock," Mrs. Lee gently prompted.

"Well, I had already tried changing the battery and that didn't do anything. So, I unscrewed the cover and noticed these plastic circles with ridges. Most of them are on," Kiara said.

"Those are gears. Did you try moving one of the clock hands and watching the gears?" Mrs. Lee asked. Kiara's eyes lit up.

"The gears move when I move the hour hand on my clock! But this one over here isn't moving at all," Kiara explained. "Maybe it is broken."

"Be sure to explore that idea, Kiara," Mrs. Lee encouraged.

After Mrs. Lee walked away, Mekhi finished changing the battery and tested his solution. Success! The calculator displayed numbers when the buttons were pushed. Kiara examined the gear and realized one of the gears was broken. She tried to make sure the gears lined up, but that didn't fix the problem because one gear kept falling apart. "I'm not sure how to put this back together," Kiara said.

"Sometimes you have to ask if you can fix it," Mrs. Lee explained. "Ask yourself the following questions: Do you have the tools you need? Do you need to take it to a special shop? Will it cost too much to fix?"

"I don't think tape would be a good idea because it would mess up the gears. Maybe some really strong glue would work," Kiara said.

"I think you should explore that idea later," Mrs. Lee told Kiara. "That way you can make sure you leave enough time for the glue to dry to test it out. You might try the glue and come back and tell us if it worked and, if it doesn't, why you think that might be. Great job figuring out what was wrong and coming up with solutions today!" Mrs. Lee said as she walked back toward the front of the classroom.

"Be sure you reconstruct your object. You wrote your steps down as you deconstructed it. Now you can follow those steps in reverse order to put it back together. Make sure it works! Once you have put your object back together, talk with your shoulder partner about what you did, if it worked, and what you learned," Mrs. Lee announced. (See Figure 2.2.)

Figure 2.2

A Scholar Gathering Pieces to Reconstruct Their Calculator

Source: Tracy Young

Source: From Cook et al., 2021.

What Is ISP 1: Use Critical and Creative Thinking to Seek Solutions

The practice standards across all the different STEM content areas (e.g., Standards for Mathematical Practice [SMPs], Science and

Engineering Practices [SEPs], and Technology and Engineering Practices [TEPs]) emphasize the importance of critical and creative thinking in solution seeking. It's important scholars have the opportunity to engage regularly in critical and creative thinking, especially as they start to build and design solutions for nonroutine real-world challenges encountered in their community and beyond. We chose to use the term *solution seeking* rather than *problem solving.* We believe the notion of problem solving is often limiting, conveying to scholars that (a) all problems can be solved and (b) problems have a definitive end. Solution seeking focuses on equipping scholars to provide or find multiple possible solutions to tasks that are captivating and challenging: captivating in the sense that scholars are interested in the topic and challenging in the sense that there is more than one solution or path to the task. This requires educators to use captivating tasks that do not have a single solution, which also helps to counteract the dominant idea that there is always one right way. Also, there are so many aspects of life where we can make positive progress, but a final or resolute solution may never be reached (such as reducing pollution, although we can never eliminate it). Helping our scholars grasp this truth while empowering them with the ownership to feel compelled to tackle these complex topics is how we make our world better for generations to come.

In this section and throughout this text, we will emphasize the importance of seeking solutions, instead of using the term *problem solving,* to convey the importance of connecting challenges to scholars' interests and to emphasize the collective solution seeking and innovating we find in integrated STEM. There are three components of this first integrated STEM practice:

1. defining and understanding challenges,

2. thinking critically for solution seeking, and

3. thinking creatively for solution innovating.

ISP 1 is called *Use Critical and Creative Thinking to Seek Solutions* because scholars are empowered as they encounter challenges that are deeply interwoven with their lives and interests and they feel individual and collective ownership to seek solutions and innovations leveraging integrated STEM.

Defining and understanding challenges requires scholars to make sense of a task so they can design a set of possible successful solutions. Scholars should ask questions to identify criteria for success and constraints placed on designing possible solutions. Criteria refers to the specific indicators by which solutions will be judged as successful or not successful.

Constraints are limitations placed on the design. Constraints can be resources (e.g., materials, time), knowledge, and costs. Defining and understanding the challenge also involves understanding the need or want inherent in the task, particularly so scholars understand how others can benefit from the solutions being presented.

As scholars progress in their abilities to define and understand challenges, they should also consider the data necessary both to design and to evaluate solutions and the forms of evidence that can be used to support potential solutions.

Critical thinking for solution seeking in STEM requires scholars to analyze, evaluate, and synthesize information through logic and reasoning skills to provide and evaluate possible solutions. Several processes exist as a model that you can draw on to guide scholars as solution seekers through critical thinking. For example, the Engineering Design Process[1] (NASA, 2018) structures scholars' thinking around

- asking questions to identify the challenges,
- imagining solutions through brainstorming,
- planning for possible solution(s),
- creating and testing the solution(s), and
- improving the solution(s).

The Design Thinking Process from Stanford (Plattner, 2010) is another model to guide critical thinking by focusing on

- empathy,
- defining problems,
- ideating,
- prototyping, and
- testing.

[1] There are many accepted and well-researched engineering design process models. We chose to use the NASA BEST engineering design model because it fits well with a majority of K–12 science curricula and with the Science and Engineering Practices in the Next Generation Science Framework.

Sometimes criteria are set by the content standards in which you are operating. Criteria can be broadened to include indicators set by the group who has created the task (e.g., community partnership).

Scholars can study the positive and negative impacts and/or influences on different populations or audiences, especially those of the global majority, for each solution presented.

Although these different models vary slightly, they all provide a helpful structure for you to facilitate your scholars' journey as they analyze, evaluate, and synthesize information to reach possible solutions by following a logical order.

Creative thinking for solution innovating in STEM requires scholars to investigate, imagine, and innovate to produce ideas based upon questioning and reasoning. When scholars are given nonroutine real-world challenges that have multiple possible solutions or paths, they are nearly called to use their creativity to seek possible solutions. This mimics the work scientists, engineers, mathematicians, and all STEM professionals do as their profession requires them to be creative in their approaches. When scholars are exposed to these nonroutine challenges, they go beyond discipline-specific applications and apply creative thinking skills as they work with ideas from across multiple disciplines. To encourage this type of creative thinking, it is important for the teacher to be "curator of opportunities and supporter of possibilities" (Brennan, 2017, p. 8), rather than leading scholars through fixed pathways. For example, rather than telling them the next step, Mrs. Lee asked scholars what other resources they could use to troubleshoot how to fix their broken item. In this way, Mrs. Lee guided them to use their own knowledge base to discern next steps and the best use of resources. Further, it empowered them to be the scholar and expert in this scenario, rather than focus on Mrs. Lee as the "qualified" expert.

Solution ideas that do not lead to the outcomes desired in the task or challenge are simply solution ideas for another task or challenge that has not yet been identified.

Critical and creative thinking are the cornerstone of ISP 1. The key idea is that there are no bad ideas throughout this process. There are only ideas that need a pivot or other improvements made to them.

Creating space in your classrooms where scholars are free to present ideas and solutions to challenges and tasks without criticism and without the drive for perfectionism is essential in implementing ISP 1.

●●● SO YOU'VE BEEN TOLD . . .

You can only teach STEM if you know all the disciplines well.

REALITY CHECK!

Not true! STEM is a team sport! At the elementary grades, teachers often teach every subject and might feel most comfortable in primarily one or two specific subjects. That's okay and expected! Remember, you aren't going at this alone! Capitalize on the knowledge of your colleagues, families, and the broader community. For example, in the story of Mrs. Lee, facilities staff could offer some tool options, or STEM-related teachers, such as the computer science or industrial technology teacher, might help brainstorm solutions, especially to really tricky ones! ●

Stop, Think, Reflect (2A)

1. How would you describe ISP 1 to a colleague?

2. How would you describe ISP 1 to a scholar who is engaging in the practice?

 Available for download at **qrs.ly/s9f1lux**

Why Does ISP 1 Matter?

Take a moment to imagine what our world would be like if we did not promote and engage scholars in critical and creative thinking. We would have no innovation. No creativity. Everything would look the same. Perform the same. Sound the same. We would all solve the same problems the same way. Life would be stagnant. The world would be pretty dull and boring.

When every scholar is given access and opportunity to use critical and creative thinking, they are empowered and have agency. They are not hedged in to think the same way, act the same way, or focus on the "right" way. Let's take a moment and consider why this is important. Scholars realize and come to understand they are essential contributors to their and others' knowledge. Their minds are vehicles to make the world better for others, themselves, and future generations. Scholars begin to become more reliant on their own reasoning and critical and creative thinking rather than the thinking of others, particularly those in positions of power such as their teachers. This helps to disrupt the system of paternalism dominance (e.g., telling scholars how to do a task or what's best, often without the scholar's input) that so often contributes to scholars' lack of a sense of belonging. Instead, scholars are empowered, positioned as qualified in their given scenarios, and vested in finding or working toward solutions. They see and begin to understand the *why* of learning because they are able to apply learning across multiple disciplines. Scholars' use of critical and creative thinking provides the stepping stones to empowerment and positive STEM identity, which are needed to become societal change agents for the communities in which they live.

Diving Deeper: Mrs. Lee as a STEM System Disruptor

In the Deconstructing and Reconstructing an Object task, Mrs. Lee engaged her second-grade scholars in using critical and creative thinking to seek solutions. By starting with an object that did not work, Mrs. Lee encouraged scholars to explain the function of the object and what was wrong with the object. Kiara and Mekhi explained their clock and calculator, respectively. They clearly defined and understood their challenges as a clock and calculator not working when they both should.

As Mrs. Lee worked with Kiara and Mekhi in the Deconstructing and Reconstructing an Object task, she directly challenged ideas of paternalism, perfectionism, and defensiveness. As scholars used their own critical and creative thinking to identify the problem with their objects, they were not relying on the ideas of others. The scholars were empowered to use their own ideas to make decisions to fix the broken objects. To address ideas of perfectionism, Mrs. Lee worked with Kiara to realize that a gear in her clock was broken and they did not have the tools to fix the gear. This did not lead to a sense of failure at the task;

instead, it is seen as a critical step in defining the problem. The conversations between Mrs. Lee, Kiara, and Mekhi also served as a model to combat defensiveness. Mrs. Lee questioned students to further their thinking. The students offered feedback to each other, such as when they shared ideas for the other person to explore. Neither student was defensive at the suggestion of a different idea.

Once the tasks were defined and understood, Mrs. Lee led scholars through an exploration where they used **critical thinking** to come up with potential solutions for their challenge.

The structured probing questions used by Mrs. Lee guided scholars through a logical thinking process to think critically. Kiara and Mekhi had to describe their object, explain how it did not work, and describe what steps they had already taken (e.g., Kiara had tried changing the batteries in her clock). Mrs. Lee also encouraged scholars to document their progress as they deconstructed their object so that they could reconstruct it later. This attention to detail is important, especially for younger scholars who are developing critical thinking skills.

This type of logical thinking also exemplifies the type of thinking we want scholars to use in mathematics when they make sense of challenges faced in our world. Scholars have to understand what the problem is asking, try a potential strategy to get the solution, and then evaluate if the strategy and solution worked or are best for the problem. As scholars engage in this type of solution seeking in many contexts, their ability to apply those skills inside and outside of the STEM classroom will be enhanced.

Mrs. Lee also intentionally reminded scholars that they were trying something new, that it might not work, and that it might take more than testing one potential solution to find something that would work. This is a necessary skill when learning technology and engineering design (International Technology and Engineering Educators

Association [ITEEA], 2020). Mrs. Lee prompted her scholars to identify something they could try and, depending on the results, continue from there or try something else. It is essential for STEM teachers to attend to the **dispositions** associated with STEM learning environments.

Perfectionism is so often the driver in our society. However, failure is an essential and expected part of the learning process and really where our scholars learn and grow. While not all of the objects would be fixed in this learning experience, forward progress was made toward a solution or next step.

Mrs. Lee also encouraged her scholars to use **creative thinking.** While critical thinking was used to diagnose the challenge, creative thinking was used to innovate and design possible solutions. Mekhi explored possible ways to fix his calculator. Creative thinking involves not just innovation but also attending to efficiency when looking at solutions.

The **utility and applicability** of this task applies to daily life as we use our STEM practices to creatively and critically identify challenges and seek different solutions to the challenges around us.

The small circular battery in Mekhi's calculator is an example of creative thinking in design because the small circular battery, which Mekhi had not seen before, was designed to provide power and conserve space in the calculator. Kiara engaged in creative thinking as she explored the gears in the clock to determine if there was a way to get them to work. Given the resources available, Kiara decided she could not fix the clock; however, exploring resources and using them in unexpected ways is a characteristic of creative thinking in STEM.

Putting ISP 1 Into Action: What Does It Look Like?

Scholars engage in critical and creative thinking to seek solutions to real-world nonroutine challenges. In Table 2.1, we describe characteristics of what a classroom would look like when the teacher and scholars engage in ISP 1.

Table 2.1

Putting ISP 1 Into Action

	ISP 1 COMPONENTS	TEACHER ACTIONS	SCHOLAR ACTIONS
ISP 1: Use critical and creative thinking to seek solutions	Defining and understanding challenges	Find, modify, or create nonroutine real-world tasks that require scholars to use knowledge from multiple disciplines and with multiple stakeholders.	Observe, question, and research ideas to define and understand the task. Identify stakeholders. Identify constraints on the design and criteria for a successful design.
	Critical thinking for solution seeking	Introduce and model a framework for critical thinking, such as the Engineering Design or Design Thinking, to encourage logical solution seeking.	Use a logical process, such as the Engineering Design or Design Thinking, to document the process used to seek solutions.
	Creative thinking for solution innovating	Encourage and model innovative uses of materials. Encourage brainstorming a variety of ideas to seek solutions to develop creative thinking skills.	Explore properties of materials and come up with nontraditional ways to use materials to seek solutions. Generate a list of ideas to seek solutions, including sketches, that can be refined later.
	Seeking solutions	Provide scaffolds for reasoning from evidence. Intentionally construct collaborative groups to dissect the learning experience.	Analyze trade-offs of proposed solutions or ideas. Consider multiple perspectives from other scholars and stakeholders.

Assessing ISP 1

Assessing critical and creative thinking can seem vague. When scholars are actively involved in critical and creative thinking activities, they are analyzing, evaluating, synthesizing, investigating, imagining, and innovating (ITEEA, 2020). In the story, Mrs. Lee used observations and purposeful questioning to assess scholars' progress. As she observed scholars, she noted what they did or did not understand. For example, when Mrs. Lee observed Mekhi looking puzzled, she stopped to have a conversation. Mrs. Lee began by asking Mekhi a purposeful, open-ended question that gave Mekhi the opportunity to revoice his current attempts at solving the challenge. When Mrs. Lee realized Mekhi was not familiar with a circular silver battery, she used the information to give Mekhi more information to help him continue solving his challenge. Mrs. Lee also took the opportunity to check in with Kiara and used a similar strategy. She asked Kiara to explain her thinking and helped further Kiara's thinking by helping her make a connection about the clock gears and the clock hands moving. Once Kiara was on the right track, Mrs. Lee did not give her more answers; instead, she encouraged her to continue exploring the idea. Mrs. Lee used these informal assessments to make instructional decisions in the moment.

Mrs. Lee also had artifacts of scholars' learning. The structured reflection tool served not only as a guide to help scholars use critical thinking to solve their problems but also as an artifact of their learning. A sample structured reflection tool for this activity is available in the online implementation toolkit. Completed forms provide information for approaches scholars used and areas where they struggled. Documenting ideas and iteratively revising them are key elements to critical thinking. Mrs. Lee could have also had scholars sketch pictures of their objects, the problem they identified with their objects, and/or solutions. Creating pictures and diagrams helps to connect creative and critical thinking—using both to try out different solutions to the challenge under investigation.

If additional resources are available, taking pictures of the objects throughout the deconstructing process and using the pictures to put together a story of the solution(s) journey is a great way to expand scholars' communication and media knowledge. This can also aid in communication if scholars are still working on communication through writing. Video documenting the process would work as well. Using a tablet, phone, or other videorecording device, a scholar could video their deconstruction process themselves or for a shoulder partner. In the video, it would be important to point out different parts of the object and how they might work together. It would also be important to point out any potential roadblocks and brainstorm ways to overcome them. Scholars could video themselves fixing the object and conduct a "failure analysis" to determine which actions have which consequences. This will help them identify next steps. Many times a solution will not work and will be considered a failure. Teachers should encourage scholars to "fail forward"—learn what worked and did not work in the failed solution and try again with a revised solution. As with all the ISPs, it is important that failure is seen as a positive part of the process and that scholars are encouraged to continue being creative and critical thinkers.

●●● SO YOU'VE BEEN TOLD . . .

Assessing STEM tasks is too complicated and time-consuming!

REALITY CHECK!

Actually, assessing scholar learning from STEM tasks is a more authentic and perhaps meaningful approach to assessment. Such an approach moves us away from procedural, surface-level multiple-choice and short-answer assessments and toward a way of offering scholars the opportunity to demonstrate their understanding in ways that more closely mirror how they will be held accountable for their knowledge in their professional and personal lives.

Assessment of STEM tasks and the ISPs encourages scholars' creativity and will better illuminate their thinking for you as the teacher, which is a win-win! In the story about Mrs. Lee's class, scholars were asked to break down the task into intentional steps, trying one potential solution to see if that worked before trying something else. Scholars asked questions and made observations about why their item didn't work and then used critical and creative thinking to fix their item. ●

In the Moment Feedback

In the Moment Feedback is a tool that educators can use as they assess scholars on ISP 1. The first set of questions are formative assessment questions meant to generate a discussion among and between you and your scholars. Such discussions will help you gain an understanding of where scholars are and what additional supports they might need as they engage in ISP 1. The Design Notebook Prompts are prompts you can provide your scholars for them to respond in writing to facilitate literacy and written communication, encourage engineering design thinking processes, and serve as a record of activity similar to what is often expected in the workforce. We encourage the use of the design notebook that showcases scholars' growth on ISP 1.

Formative Assessment Questions (teachers asking scholars)

Purpose: In the Moment Feedback

- What are some potential challenges or limitations with this learning experience? What are your ideas for overcoming them?

- What's a unique way that might not have been tried before in this learning experience?

- If you had unlimited resources, what ideas would you have for seeking a solution for this learning experience?

- Have you seen a similar task before? If so, where? What solutions do you think they tried?

Design Notebook Prompts (scholars complete individually or in groups)

Purpose: Continuous record of learning experiences/final showcase of work

- When I first saw this task, I thought _____. I had the following questions about the task (list at least two questions).

  _____

  _____

  _____

  _____

- If you had unlimited resources, an idea for a solution for this learning experience is _____. What resources would you need for this solution?

  _____

  _____

- The most unusual solution for this learning experience would be _____. What makes it unusual?

  _____

  _____

- List the ideas you generated for the experience.

  _____

  _____

  _____

  _____

- Indicate if these ideas are sustainable or not sustainable.

  _____

  _____

  _____

  _____

- Pick one idea that is sustainable and explain why.

  _____

  _____

- Pick one idea that is not sustainable and explain why.

  _____

  _____

ISP 1 RUBRIC

In Table 2.2, we provide a rubric that you can use to assess your scholars' engagement in ISP 1.

Table 2.2

ISP 1 Rubric

ISP 1 COMPONENTS	NEEDS MORE SUPPORT	APPROACHES EXPECTATION	MEETS EXPECTATION	ACHIEVING SOCIETAL CHANGE AGENT
Identifying the challenge (Critical Thinking)	Challenge and context are not yet mentioned. It is unclear what is being investigated.	Challenge is vaguely defined. Context may or may not be present. While a broken or nonfunctioning object is present, it is vague regarding the challenge.	Challenge is specifically defined for the project. The criteria for how the object is supposed to work are clearly defined. Constraints are somewhat considered.	Challenge is specifically defined as well as the constraints. Goals for the object are specific and able to be tested.
Identifying solutions (Creative Thinking)	Only one solution is constructed for the challenge.	Describes a few solutions but it's not yet clear how they will be carried out.	Describes multiple solutions with a plan for how to carry them out. For example, ranking how the solutions should be approached.	Describes multiple solutions with justifications. Understands the constraints of the solutions and has a plan for carrying them out.
Testing and revising solutions (Critical and Creative Thinking)	Solution is not yet tested or there is no plan for testing.	Tests and makes changes to solutions, but there is not yet a clear path to the ultimate solution. The different trials do not yet build on each other or prior results.	Uses an iterative process to test different solutions. Carefully documents and plans each test based on the results of the previous test.	Uses an iterative process to test different solutions, taking into consideration each previous test and additional constraints learned along the way. The process is carefully documented.

1. How could you use ISP 1 in your own classroom?

2. How could you turn a current lesson into one that engages scholars with ISP 1?

 Available for download at **qrs.ly/s9f1lux**

 **Recap This!**

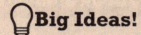 **Big Ideas!**

ISP 1

Use Critical and Creative Thinking to Seek Solutions

The most meaningful STEM tasks are deeply interwoven with scholars' lives and interests, and they feel individual and collective ownership to seek solutions and innovations. Engaging in ISP 1 enables scholars to see the **utility** and **applicability** of STEM in the world around them.	Critical thinking for solution seeking in STEM requires scholars to analyze, evaluate, and synthesize information through logic and reasoning skills to provide potential solutions. When scholars engage in **critical thinking** to seek solutions, they become **empowered** and see themselves as agents of change.
Creative thinking for solution innovating in STEM requires scholars to investigate, imagine, and innovate to produce ideas based upon questioning and reasoning. Being engaged in the solution-seeking process develops scholars' positive **dispositions in STEM** and enables them to see themselves as makers and doers of STEM.	Don't wait to engage your scholars as solution seekers! **Solution seeking** and engaging in ISP 1 serves as ways to develop STEM content, practices, and skills in your scholars.

●●● STEM STARTERS

• Your work planning an ISP learning experience will be primarily on the front end. Once you begin implementing, your scholars will be the ones doing the hard work (critical and creative thinking), as they should be!

- Instead of adding to your plate, the ISPs help streamline your efforts! The ISPs aren't an add-on. The ISPs are a strategic tool for addressing existing standards in a more high-quality (and more efficient) way.

- Not only does considering STEM through an ISP lens provide focus and direction to your STEM efforts, but embodying the ISPs ensures scholars have access to the types of STEM tasks they rightfully deserve.

- Adopting the ISPs and implementing them intentionally is a commitment to equity, access, and a strengths-based approach to instruction!

Questions to Ponder /Book Study Prompts

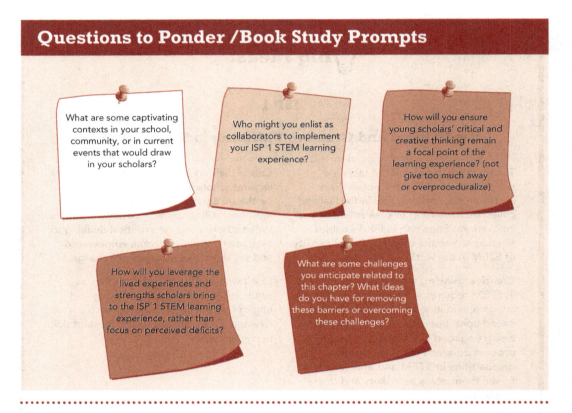

What are some captivating contexts in your school, community, or in current events that would draw in your scholars?

Who might you enlist as collaborators to implement your ISP 1 STEM learning experience?

How will you ensure young scholars' critical and creative thinking remain a focal point of the learning experience? (not give too much away or overproceduralize)

How will you leverage the lived experiences and strengths scholars bring to the ISP 1 STEM learning experience, rather than focus on perceived deficits?

What are some challenges you anticipate related to this chapter? What ideas do you have for removing these barriers or overcoming these challenges?

online resources — Available for download at **qrs.ly/s9f1lux**

TRY THIS!

Whether you're trying a new STEM task or reimagining one you've used in the past, try the following in Table 2.3 to highlight the aspects of ISP 1 we have discussed in this chapter.

Table 2.3

ISP 1: Use Critical and Creative Thinking to Seek Solutions

COMPONENTS TO ISP 1	ASPECTS OF TASK	QUESTION PROMPTS FOR SCHOLARS
Define and Understand Challenges	Make authentic connections	How does this connect to your life?
	Identify criteria and constraints	What specific goals (criteria) and limitations (constraints) do you have?
	Be clear about connections to mathematics, science, technology, and engineering	How did you use ideas of science and mathematics to help you seek solutions to this task?
Critical Thinking	Identify important information	What information is needed as you work to approach this task?
	Apply logic to solution seeking	If you could change one aspect or variable, what would change?
	Consider multiple perspectives	Who else is impacted by this issue? In what ways might other people perceive the issue differently?
Creativity	Encourage exploration of materials	What types of tools do you need? What might these tools offer? What are the limitations of the tools we have?
	Allow time for brainstorming a variety of ideas	What are some other ideas you could try?
	Embrace mistakes	What did you learn from taking risks? What did you learn when your idea did not work?
Seek Solutions	Probe for reasoning	Why did this solution seem like the best approach?
	Consider trade-offs	For this solution, what were the trade-offs you had to make?
	Structure collaborative groups for diverse thinking	What unique contributions did each group member make?

CHAPTER 3

ISP 2: COLLABORATE AND USE APPROPRIATE TOOLS TO ENGAGE IN ITERATIVE DESIGN

In the following story, you will meet Mx. Thompson, a fifth-grade teacher who engages their scholars in the ISP of collaborating and using appropriate tools for iterative design. As you read, look for . . .

- How Mx. Thompson facilitates the scholars' collaborative use of tools to engage in iterative design

- How the scholars collaborate and use tools to engage in iterative design

- Ways this learning experience provides opportunities for collaborating and using tools to engage in iterative design

●●● THE STORY OF MX. THOMPSON

Mx. Thompson (they/them) had been teaching fifth-grade science for years and wanted to try something new with their unit on energy. They knew their fifth graders enjoyed hands-on inquiries, so Mx. Thompson decided they would try out a roller coaster design challenge to teach the concepts of force, motion, mass, and speed. While they found many existing plans for roller coaster design, Mx. Thompson wanted to ensure they were highlighting the integrated STEM practices their district was talking so much about related to collaboration and design. Mx. Thompson also anticipated that some scholars had never had the opportunity to ride or see a roller coaster in person and took this into account in their planning and implementation of the task.

On the first day of their energy unit, Mx. Thompson asked their scholars to brainstorm the feelings that came to mind when thinking of roller coasters. Mx. Thompson played a video that provided an overview of different types of roller coasters so that all scholars had background knowledge about different types of roller coasters. They asked their scholars what they thought it would feel like when going through all the twists, turns, and sudden drops. Next, Mx. Thompson asked their scholars to respond to a few preassessment questions to gauge their understanding of the science behind roller coasters. They asked, "How does the mass of an object impact its movement when a force is exerted?" For this question, scholars were reminded of ideas of weathering and erosion they learned about in earlier grades. Several scholars recalled that larger rocks took more force to move than smaller rocks, particularly when considering the amount of wind or water it took to move large rocks versus small rocks. Although they were touching on ideas of force and motion, scholars did not at this point use formal scientific concepts to explain their ideas.

Mx. Thompson then asked, "How would we define speed?" Almost all scholars focused on how fast an object moves, relating it to cars that go so many miles per hour. "And what specific things do you think we look at when we think about speed? Specifically, think about the miles per hour many of you just mentioned. What are some measurable components in miles per hour?" Mx. Thompson wanted scholars to understand the definition that speed is calculated by determining distance traveled in a period of time. So, when the open question prompt of "So, how does a roller coaster slow down and speed up?" was posed, scholars buzzed with ideas about what they had seen and experienced. For example, one scholar recalled there was a chain that she watched as the roller coaster was pulled up a hill. During this preassessment time, Mx. Thompson noticed excitement building as scholars wanted to share their experiences and try to explain how they thought roller coasters worked.

With the anticipation building, Mx. Thompson told scholars they were going to work in groups to create a model of a roller coaster. Specifically, they would use the materials available to design a roller coaster that relied on gravity to move a marble. It was time to dive into the investigation of designing fun, safe, and affordable roller coasters (these were the criteria with which Mx. Thompson set the stage for the inquiry). Scholars had an open discussion to operationalize what each criterion meant. For example, "fun" was defined as fast with lots of hills and loops. "Safe" meant the riders needed to be protected with no sudden jerks that might hurt them. "Affordable" meant scholars needed to know how much their designs would cost and work within a prescribed budget. This led Mx. Thompson to the constraints present in the model building, which included materials, budget, and time. Mx. Thompson showed scholars the materials they would have available to them, which included foam insulation cut in half lengthwise to simulate a track and various sized marbles made of different materials meant to represent the riders. There were different types of tape available and many smaller items such as cotton balls, sandpaper, rubber strips, and cups. While all groups would receive a stopwatch and measuring tape at "no cost," Mx. Thompson told scholars they needed to work within their budget and determine which of the other materials they felt were necessary to purchase. This required scholars to flexibly use decimal operations to craft and revise their budget as they considered properties of the different materials they could use to create their designs.

When determining group roles, teachers might allow scholars to determine the job descriptions. Oftentimes, scholars will come up with unique job descriptions that can allow them to contribute to the group project in meaningful ways.

Scholars were grouped into design teams of three. Creating design teams encouraged scholars to make sense of multiple perspectives in their team's design. Each scholar was expected to contribute ideas for the design and was given the opportunity to choose a role to maintain during the task:

1) Materials manager: responsible for maintaining the group's official budget and materials list based off of each group member's individual contributions

2) Data analyst: responsible for recording and summarizing the results of each test of the model with support from other group members

3) Community advocate: responsible for taking the information from the trials and, with support from the other group members, advocating for an outcome based on the data

Allowing scholars to choose their roles encouraged them to contribute valuable skills for coordination of the group and provided clear expectations for group work. Mx. Thompson's district had been talking about effective collaboration and the importance of scholars' sense of belonging in their learning. They knew this task offered an opportunity for scholars to select the role they were most interested in and showcase their skill sets through different roles within the inquiry. They wanted to ensure equitable participation through rich and meaningful roles—ones that required intellectual rigor and were authentically connected to the inquiry (Wood et al., 2019). Mx. Thompson also knew they needed to spend time with the scholars, ensuring they knew the expectations for each role clearly and to offer time for self-reflection on team contributions.

Over the course of six 30-minute blocks, scholars designed and built their roller coasters and tested them for fun (based on speed). Mx. Thompson noticed that groups wanted to dive right into building the roller coasters and that initial tests resulted in the marble "riders" being flung from the coaster. Mx. Thompson asked the group, "Why do you think the rider fell off?" and "What could be done to slow the rider down?" Concepts such as changes in speed or direction required a force and are affected by mass naturally emerged as different solutions to the problem. Mx. Thompson reminded scholars to test only one change at a time and that the data analyst needed to document the effect on speed of each change. For example, groups tested adding sandpaper versus a rubber strip on the track to slow the rider. Others chose to use a lower rise in the drop to lessen the potential energy in the system. Scholars applied knowledge of division to calculate the speed (*speed = distance ÷ time*) at which the marble completed the roller coaster track. One group tested whether adding guardrails on the track would impact whether the rider would stay safely on the track. Another group tested the differences between using a steel versus a glass marble to test the effect of mass on speed. Groups were engaged in iterative design as they continued to test their prototypes and refine them based on data. As Mx. Thompson moved around the groups, they had scholars verbally describe the force and motion in their design. (See Figure 3.1.)

Figure 3.1

Scholars Refer to Their Sketches as They Begin Creating Their Roller Coasters

Source: Julie Sick-Panus

Groups noted the data by recording speed for design changes and drawing schematics of their roller coaster in their design notebook. They revised their budget each time they changed the materials they needed. Materials managers documented properties of the materials used in the roller coaster design. For example, in their design notebook, one scholar noted how another group used "sticky" strips to slow down the marble at the end of the track, which allowed the marble to come to a complete and smooth stop—contributing to the safety of the ride. Data analysts recorded notes and data from each test of the model and led the group in discussion about what they noticed from the data after each test. Community advocates were expected to communicate changes and progress. Before each community advocate reported their results and provided evidence to back up the claims that their design was fun, safe, and affordable, teams took a gallery walk around the room to review one another's designs. Once groups reconvened, they discussed what they noticed in other designs and took notes of other teams' design choices. Importantly, the community advocate also conducted research and facilitated their team's discussion on how to make roller coasters more accessible. This included strategies for how the community could ensure every scholar in the school had an opportunity to see STEM in action—through seeing roller coasters in person! It also included strategies for building community awareness around lack of access, educational benefits including career connections, raising money and resources for ensuring access, and a plan to put it into motion.

In order to assess scholars' progress, Mx. Thompson offered scholars a menu of assessment options. Although they could choose which items they wished to complete for the assessment, all items addressed the same or similar elements. In effect, whether they were writing a news story about why a roller coaster design failed, for example, or creating and performing a skit to describe the forces at play in the system, in all situations, scholars were expected to showcase their understanding of force and motion, mass, and speed. In addition, scholars were to specifically describe how the mathematics such as the changes in speed contributed to the design, decision-making, and solution-seeking process.

At the end of the task, Mx. Thompson was pleased with the use of the roller coaster unit to teach the physical science concepts they wanted scholars to explore. Moreover, they were excited that placing intentional focus on collaboration and strategic solution seeking resulted in scholars' engagement and a rich learning experience for all. ●

Source: From Cook, et al., 2017.

It's too complicated and messy to teach more than one or two content standards at a time.

REALITY CHECK!

That is simply not true. Integrating multiple content standards at the same time can give scholars more meaningful experiences with the content. In the end, teaching more than one standard at a time through these types of ISP tasks could in fact save you time! The key is integrating them in authentic, meaningful, and seamless ways. Force-fitting standards just to check off a list is counterproductive. Instead, we argue that integrating multiple STEM practices and content standards, as you can see from the ISP 2 story of Mx. Thompson, can be clear and simple in implementation when the practices and content are indeed needed to seek solutions. In the story of Mx. Thompson, multiple mathematics and science practices and content standards were addressed, which ended up being a simple, transparent, and more effective use of time. Most important, it provided a meaningful and powerful learning experience for scholars. ●

What Is ISP 2: Collaborate and Use Appropriate Tools to Engage in Iterative Design

In the second integrated STEM practice, scholars collaborate to use the most appropriate tools to plan, test, and refine their solutions to nonroutine real-world challenges. There are three components of this second integrated STEM practice:

1. collaboration,

2. using appropriate tools, and

3. the iterative nature of design.

At the heart of this practice—and across all of the integrated STEM practices and the STEM fields—is collaboration. Collaboration helps to develop effective communication skills, encourages solution seeking, promotes inclusion, and enhances teamwork. Collaboration requires scholars to communicate effectively with other scholars and stakeholders. While collaborating, scholars learn how to listen to all voices, find voices that may be left out, articulate their own ideas, and provide feedback to their peers' ideas. While scholars are listening to stakeholders, conducting their research together around possible solutions, they are also learning from each other and learning to appreciate each other's differences. Collaboration allows for the exchange of ideas and feedback among and across team members. This can ultimately lead to the development of more creative and effective solutions. Finally, collaboration requires scholars to work as a team toward a common goal. Working as a team can look different depending on the grade level and expectations within each group of scholars. Some important things to consider when setting scholars up for success in regard to collaboration include the following:

- Does the team understand the common goal?
  - Have scholars independently write in their design notebooks what they think the common goal is. Then, have them share within their team. If scholars agree, have them collectively define what the goal is and write it down in their design notebooks.

- What are the norms in your educational setting for managing conflicts?
  - It's unrealistic to think or encourage scholars to not have conflict when collaborating together. Rather, it's important to share upfront with scholars what managing conflict looks like in a collaborative setting. Sometimes this can happen through a common set of norms that are created commonly in the education setting, or it can be a common set of norms the scholars create together. Rather than instilling a fear of conflict, it's important to share that conflict will happen during collaboration, and we can work together to achieve resolution during the conflict. It's important to directly address defensiveness during conflict resolution. Actively listening and taking ownership of one's actions can proactively help to overcome defensiveness when managing conflict in collaborative settings.

- What roles are the scholars playing within each team?
  - In order to ensure equity among the collaborative team, it's important that each scholar has a role and that they understand their role. Roles can be preassigned or they can be created within the team once the task is assigned.

Roles do not have to be static, but rather, they can change among the scholars so everyone gets a turn, or they can be fluid as the needs of the task changes. It's important to consider the different areas of the task and where scholars can provide expertise and contribute the most value. Ensuring understood roles within a team also helps to create efficiency and effectiveness, especially toward achieving the common goal of the task.

- What does supporting each other look like?
  - Scholars supporting each other can look different depending on the educational setting, the expectations, and grade level or age. Scholars should be encouraged to share multiple creative ideas, rather than one right way or having one (dominant voice) idea as important. If a scholar is stuck, having another scholar help generate ideas or directly aid the scholar in getting unstuck helps to show empathy. Finally, scholars support each other with respectful and positive language.

Overall, cultivating effective collaborations among scholars helps to prepare them for success in future settings, their careers, and beyond. It also helps to foster a love for learning and an appreciation for the importance of working together to solve complex problems.

Through the iterative design process, scholars collaborate together to bring their ideas, perspectives, and knowledge to develop and try out solutions. Iterative design involves a process of creating, testing, and refining a product, model, idea, solution, and so on through multiple cycles. While we encourage creativity and innovation within the iterative design process, it's important to help scholars keep focused on creating solutions to try out rather than trying to create the most perfect and innovative solution. Perfectionism can kill the iterative design process.

When beginning a new task toward a defined common goal, it's important to generate lots of ideas and possibilities. Collaboration tools such as whiteboards, online brainstorming web applications, and group discussions can be used to encourage sharing and discussion of ideas. If conducting group discussions for idea generating, encourage scholars to first spend some independent time thinking through possible ideas and solutions and writing them down in the design notebooks. This encourages and empowers scholars to generate their own ideas and not rely on others to generate the ideas and solutions. During the brainstorming and ideation process, scholars may want to access online research tools or library research tools that will allow them to explore relevant background information and existing solutions.

Once the team has identified potential solutions, it's important to create models or prototypes and test them in a variety of ways. This will look different depending on the constraints of your educational setting. Appropriate tools such as CAD (computer-aided design) software, 3D printers, sensors, and physical models can be used to create and test out prototypes or models. If the solution does not involve a physical model, online simulations can be conducted to iteratively test the solutions.

As the team tests and refines their model or prototypes, it's important to gather feedback from peers and external stakeholders. This can be difficult for teams as they may want to get defensive of their ideas. However, this is where the norm setting around managing conflict can be useful. It's important to reiterate to scholars that the purpose of the feedback is to improve their models, prototypes, or solutions. Having a standard way to give feedback is beneficial. When providing feedback to peers, scholars can frame their feedback in the following ways:

- I have a question about . . . State the question. → This is useful when asking questions of fact to clarify the purpose or component of the prototype.

- I like . . . → It's important to give feedback on what scholars like about the prototype. What do they think is working well? What should the team consider keeping in the prototype?

- I wonder . . . → Instead of stating "I think you should do this differently" or "I think you should change," have scholars phrase their feedback for a change idea in terms of an *I wonder* statement. *I wonder* statements help scholars to listen to the words of the change idea. It can also generate a conversation about the idea rather than presenting it solely as a change. Finally, it helps peers to learn how to give constructive feedback in a way that will be listened to and received by the presenting team.

You can also use your favorite critique or tuning protocol if you already have one (see https://my.pblworks.org/resource/critique-protocols). While the feedback portion is important, even more critical is the opportunity for refinement based on trials and feed-back. Constraints within the educational setting may limit the iterative design process, especially the number of iterations there is time and space to complete; therefore, at least two refinement cycles are encouraged with each task.

Finally, throughout the process, it's important to document the iterative design process. We recommend using a design notebook. If using a digital design notebook, it's important scholars have access to free-form drawing tools that allow them to sketch their ideas and models.

Throughout the iterative design process, scholars should have access to a variety of tools that can help them in creating and try-ing out their solutions or ideas. Using appropriate tools can help scholars to generate new ideas and test solutions more effectively and efficiently. The key is to use the right tool for the challenge and to be open to new ideas and approaches. Of course, there are limitations to the right tool for the challenge, including, but not limited to, cost, availability, age appropriateness, safety, and so on. What is the right tool for the challenge? Any kind of tool that helps scholars in creating, testing, and improving their ideas and solutions toward achieving their common goal. Appropriate tools can be a broad range of items or access points. The following list are some general areas and ideas to consider when thinking about appropriate tools.

- Physical tools—markers, colored pencils, colored paper, cardboard, tape, staples, empty toilet paper rolls, toothpicks, wooden skewers, protractor, ruler, pencils

- Physical modeling tools—cardboard, cardstock, balsa wood, glue, wood glue, hot or cool glue guns, tape, duct tape, re-stickable paper, posterboard, large spaces to create (floor, large rooms)

- Computer modeling tools—3D printing, CNC (computer numerical control) machining, web applications that allow for 3D creating and modeling, auto-CAD (computer-added design) software or web applications, simulation software

- Data analysis tools—spreadsheets, collaborative spreadsheets, calculators, online graphing calculators

- Collaboration tools—design notebooks, tasks lists, roles lists, spreadsheets

- Science and mathematics tools—microscopes, spectrometers, rulers, scales, burners, goggles, online databases, dynamic geometry software, probability simulators, calculators, online graphing calculators, spreadsheets

Appropriate tools can be preidentified by the educational leader. This can especially be considered when there are time constraints, tools constraints, and so on. Other times, appropriate tools can be identified and requested by the scholars. You could even consider a budget for tools for the scholars to purchase and use.

By using appropriate tools strategically, scholars can learn to be efficient, gain deeper insights, and continue to develop and practice valuable critical thinking and solution-seeking skills. See Figure 3.2.

Educational leaders play an important role because they can help provide opportunity and access to the tools essential for scholars to use, provide guidance and feedback on appropriate tools to use,

Figure 3.2

Scholars Collaborate to Use a Tool to Measure the Angle Before Launching a Rocket

Source: Julie Sicks-Panus

and help to regularly integrate the tools in a purposeful and intentional way. See Figure 3.3.

Collaboration and the use of appropriate tools throughout the iterative design process in STEM helps teams to share ideas, divide tasks, test and refine solutions, and document progress. By working collaboratively and using appropriate tools, scholars continue to hone their knowledge and skills, especially toward creating ideas and solutions when seeking solutions to integrated STEM tasks.

Figure 3.3

Scholars Use a Schematic and Tools to Safely Create Cookie Cutters

Source: Julie Sick-Panus

Stop, Think, Reflect (3A) ✔

1. How would you describe ISP 2 to a colleague?

2. How would you describe ISP 2 to a scholar engaging in the practice?

 Available for download at **qrs.ly/s9f1lux**

Why Does ISP 2 Matter?

Consider the following scenario. You have meticulously organized your to-do list and you are ready to get started on a task. You read the first item: cut the grass. You look outside and gasp at how quickly and tall the grass has grown. You put on your shoes and sunglasses, grab your clippers, and head outside. You stand outside and gaze at the lawn. You kneel down on the edge of the lawn and begin cutting the grass with the clippers.

Source: Istock.com/SomeSense

As you finish clipping a small section of the lawn, you inch over to work on another section. After an hour of cutting, you stand up and look at the lawn in bewilderment. You only *mowed* an eighth of the lawn! You shake your head realizing it will take an additional 7 hours to finish. Unbelievable! You look at your clippers, then at the lawn, and back at your clippers. A neighbor stops by and offers to help. You tell them to grab a pair of clippers and thank them for offering to help. You both continue *mowing* the lawn for another 2 hours before taking a break.

Source: istock.com/SomeSense; istock.com/Tevarak

During your break, you walk past the shed to get a glass of water. After drinking some water, you go inside the shed and lean against the wall to take a breather. You notice a shiny aluminum lawn mower in the middle of the shed. You and your neighbor begin sharing how the lawn mower would be a more appropriate tool to use to *mow* the lawn. You push the lawn mower out of the shed and complete mowing the lawn.

Source: istock.com/cjp

While this scenario is a bit absurd, it is essential to reflect on, even in its absurdity, the importance of collaboration and using appropriate tools when seeking solutions.

When we provide space and time for our scholars to collaborate with one another, they have the opportunity to gain and deepen their own understanding, as well as enrich the understanding of their peers. We do not learn in isolation. We learn, grow, and thrive in collaboration with one another. When we have space for our scholars to collaborate, they build off of each other's ideas, thoughts, and strategies. They have the space to discuss what is and is not working as they are seeking solutions when working toward solving various challenges. We all have heard the cliche, multiple brains are better than one. In reality, this could not be more true. When scholars with multiple ideas and diverse thoughts collaborate and have their voices heard, they have the opportunity to make sense of these varied ideas and work toward creating a plan to gather evidence and to draw conclusions. Based on the conclusions they draw, scholars can refine their plan and retest their ideas to see if stronger conclusions result. Why is this important? It is important for scholars to not accept things at face value. It is important for them to collaborate with one another, to plan, to test, and to draw conclusions, as well as to refine, retest, and draw new conclusions. This process supports a more just society where we are not relying on a single entity or entities to do the thinking for us, but we are thinking for ourselves. Further, collaborating helps scholars to see the world from viewpoints outside their own lived experiences. This type of collaboration and communication fosters empathy and is generative toward building a sense of urgency.

Scholars have to be equipped to be advocates and change-makers in service of a more equitable and just world. In order to do this, scholars must be equipped to think for themselves and work together to solve challenges they will encounter in their lives. Our scholars are empowered to do so by collaboratively using appropriate tools in their planning, testing, drawing conclusions, refining, testing, and drawing new conclusions. As you can see, ISP 2 is a lifelong practice.

Stop, Think, Reflect (3B)

1. How did you see Mx. Thompson engage scholars in ISP 2? What specific actions did they use throughout the task?

2. How was the collaboration structured to maximize the learning experience?

3. How were appropriate tools selected for the task?

4. In what ways was the iterative nature of design evident?

 Available for download at **qrs.ly/s9f1lux**

●●● SO YOU'VE BEEN TOLD . . .

If I integrate the STEM disciplines, I will lose the mathematics and science.

REALITY CHECK!

Integrating STEM and bringing out the ISPs actually reveals the content more deeply. ISP 2 focuses on collaborating and using appropriate tools to seek solutions. In the story of Mx. Thompson, when scholars engaged in ISP 2, they were allowed to test one change at a time as they worked toward their optimal roller coaster design choices. Scholars took an authentic, interdisciplinary approach, seamlessly using content and the practices to consider, test, revise, and retest their designs. In addition to the practice standards aligned earlier in this chapter, mathematics content included making revisions to the variables of speed and using algebraic reasoning and rise and run (informally). The scholars engaged in mathematics content of reasoning and flexibly using decimal operations to make decisions around a budget simultaneously with the science concepts of force and motion around speed, direction, force, circular motion, effects of mass and speed, and potential energy. Through ISP 2 and integrated STEM, scholars had a powerful and meaningful experience engaging in mathematics and science practices as well as content, much more so than what would have occurred with a contrived activity. So, in reality, nothing was lost, but so much was gained! ●

Diving Deeper: Mx. Thompson as a STEM System Disruptor

In the Designing a Roller Coaster task, scholars collaborated with their groups to iteratively solve problems as they attempted to improve their roller coaster designs. Mx. Thompson challenged the ideas of qualified and power hoarding that help maintain the STEM status quo. Mx. Thompson facilitated a discussion to operationalize the criteria. This positions scholars as competent contributors to the process. They also challenged ideas of power hoarding by having a structured system for collaboration, where each scholar actively contributes to the group.

With a series of challenges, scholars worked toward a common goal of a safe, affordable, and fun design. Scholars explored ideas of trade-offs, important in engineering design, and budgeting. As scholars faced constraints of a limited budget and limited materials, they naturally applied mathematical reasoning as they considered trade-offs in selecting materials for their designs. This also required scholars to flexibly use their mathematical knowledge to update their budgets as they made decisions about materials for their fun, affordable, and safe design. With each test run, scholars had to identify the next challenge to be solved (i.e., too fast, marble fell off the track, marble could

not make it around the loop). Each of these opportunities throughout the design process allowed groups to **think critically and seek solutions** in order to assess their ideas and make incremental improvements.

Mx. Thompson intentionally ensured scholars captured each of their refinements in their design notebook. This was an important step to facilitating an iterative design process. Oftentimes, scholars will try to make several tweaks all at once without thinking about the purpose and expectations that go into each change. By logging the changes they made to the roller coaster, scholars were able to observe specific results from each change.

Because each member of the team had a specific job to do, their sense of belonging in the group was palpable. Scholars did not want to miss the action of the design, which resulted in accountability in their role to the rest of the team. As such, each

scholar's **STEM identity development** was supported as part of the experience.

Scholars drew on their strengths as a materials manager, data analyst, or community advocate to contribute to the team effort. Moreover, scholars were thinking like engineers and doing the work of a designer. Beyond keeping them engaged, scholars' roles gave them the authentic experience of working as part of a solution-seeking, collaborative team. Further, after engaging in the collaboration and design, the community advocate brought their team together around a common cause—to develop a proposal to increase access to theme park experiences. Because the design challenge drew on specific concepts within mathematics and science, scholars had to draw in and develop content

and skills relevant to the need-to-knows of the moment. By engaging in this STEM learning experience, scholars see the **utility and applicability** of the STEM disciplines related to what they are learning.

Scholars are not confined to only working on the embedded mathematics or the science behind force and motion—instead, they are fluidly using the knowledge and skills that are needed for the task at hand. For example, when describing the "fun factor" of their roller coaster, scholars calculated the speed and communicated the authentic mathematical concepts needed to describe the rider experience. Scholars authentically drew on the necessary concepts and practices to showcase their ideas and defend the claim that their design was an intentional one. Teachers often find that scholars who do not believe they are good at mathematics or who claim they do not like science often become highly engaged in these authentic learning experiences in which the design challenge drives the inquiry, and the embedded mathematics and science is an organic part of the task. When these experiences become commonplace, positive shifts in scholars' STEM identities and sense of belonging can begin to happen.

Incorporating access and equity considerations into STEM learning experiences will take time away from the practices and content, and there just isn't enough time.

REALITY CHECK!

As we can see from the story of Mx. Thompson, a key component of ISP 2 was to ensure that all scholars had some knowledge of theme parks and roller coasters. Accessibility to all in the community, whether an individual chooses to ride them or not, was a key component of this ISP 2 task. Considering equitable access didn't take time away from STEM practices and content. Instead, considering opportunities to ensure access to actual lived experiences gives meaning to the practices and content being learned and applied. Having scholars consider context and engaging as community advocates generates empathy and motivation for STEM learning. It creates the spark! STEM learning will have limited impact if it's not meaningful and applicable to the lives of scholars. ●

Putting ISP 2 Into Action: What Does It Look Like?

Scholars collaborate and use appropriate tools to plan, test, and refine their solutions to real-world nonroutine challenges. In Table 3.1, we describe what engagement in ISP 2 would look like in a classroom.

Table 3.1

Putting ISP 2 Into Action

	ISP 2 COMPONENTS	TEACHER ACTIONS	SCHOLAR ACTIONS
ISP 2: Collaborate and use appropriate tools to engage in iterative design	Collaboration	Define roles and responsibilities to ensure every scholar is participating. Offer self-reflection opportunities to examine roles throughout the learning.	Maintain assigned or chosen role. Self-reflect on role and responsibility.

(Continued)

(Continued)

	ISP 2 COMPONENTS	TEACHER ACTIONS	SCHOLAR ACTIONS
ISP 2: Collaborate and use appropriate tools to engage in iterative design (continued)	Collaboration (continued)	Define conflict management strategies. Ensure scholars have an understanding of the common goal of the task.	Show respect and support toward each other. Practice conflict management strategies when necessary.
	Use of appropriate tools	Provide materials but require scholars to have a rationale for their use. Define criteria and constraints of the challenge. Ensure material options are accessible to every scholar and team.	Choose tools needed for a specific task and provide rationale for use of tools. Understand why some tools are superior to others for a task. Ask for tools needed with a rationale if they are not already provided.
	Iterative design	Demonstrate and support a systematic approach to solution seeking by focusing on one variable at a time. Provide opportunities for documenting design and redesign. Encourage different starting points and approaches to launching the design process—this makes entering the task more accessible. Provide intentional opportunities for peer feedback and use prompts to help guide the feedback process.	Record iterative design process in a design notebook, including results of tests, peer feedback, and change ideas. Use test results and peer feedback to refine designs. Identify the need-to-knows for task. Analyze trade-offs for a proposed solution. Provide constructive feedback to peers on ideas and solutions. Receive constructive feedback from peers on ideas and solutions without being defensive.

Assessing ISP 2

Similar to Mrs. Lee in Chapter 2, Mx. Thompson used observations and purposeful questioning to assess scholars' progress. Mx. Thompson focused on using questions as a way to preassess scholars' knowledge, build interest in the task, and make clear connections to content. Mx. Thompson also used questions to help scholars engage in iterative design, such as when they asked a group why the rider fell off and what changes they could make to slow the rider down. This guided questioning did not restrict scholars' creativity or solutions but focused their efforts on aspects related to criteria for success with the task.

Mx. Thompson also used scholars' artifacts of learning. Scholars were expected to record their thinking in design notebooks. This included their brainstorming, mathematical thinking, schematics, and data they collected and analyzed when testing their designs. The journaling in their design notebooks helped scholars see the applicability of discipline-specific content as they could use concepts from mathematics and science to inform their designs. Mx. Thompson also provided choice in how scholars demonstrated their learning. Some groups wrote a news story about why the roller coaster design failed while others performed a skit describing the forces at play within the system. The choice allowed scholars to demonstrate their learning in modalities that leveraged their strengths.

In the Moment Feedback

In the Moment Feedback is a tool that educators can use as they are assessing scholars on ISP 2. The first set of questions are formative assessment questions meant to generate a discussion among and between you and your scholars. You will be able to get an understanding of where scholars are and what other supports they might need as they engage in ISP 2. The Design Notebook Prompts are prompts you can provide your scholars for them to respond in writing to facilitate literacy and written communication, encourage engineering design thinking processes, and serve as a record of activity similar to what is expected in the workforce. We encourage the use of the design notebook that showcases scholars' growth on ISP 2.

Formative Assessment Questions (teachers asking scholars)

Purpose: In the Moment Feedback

- What tool(s) did you decide to use? Why did you use that tool(s)? Were there other tools you considered?

- How did the tools or technology enhance or hinder your learning and solution-seeking process?

- How did you define how you would work together? Were there others left out in your approach? How did you include them or how could you include them?

- How do you feel communication is helping your teams' ability to complete the task successfully? What questions do you have for your peers about where you are with the task?

- How successful have your trials been in giving you feedback toward your solution?

Design Notebook Prompts (scholars complete individually or in groups)

Purpose: Continuous record of learning experiences/final showcase of work

- The tool I/we found most useful in completing this task was . . . This is because . . . (why).

- I learned _____ from my peers when working on this task.

- I faced _____ challenge when working with others on this task. I/we overcame it by _____.

- I/we made _____ changes throughout the iterative design process. The change that most impacted my final solution or product was _____.

 Available for download at **qrs.ly/s9f1lux**

ISP 2 RUBRIC

In Table 3.2, we provide a rubric that you can use to assess your scholars' engagement in ISP 2.

Table 3.2

ISP 2 Rubric

ISP 2 COMPONENTS	NEEDS MORE SUPPORT	APPROACHES EXPECTATION	MEETS EXPECTATION	ACHIEVING SOCIETAL CHANGE AGENT
Common understanding of task (Collaboration)	There is no common understanding of the goal of the task.	While able to describe the task, unable to describe the goal of the task.	Describes the goal of the task.	Describes the goal of the task and assists peers in ensuring they have the same understanding of the goal.
Conflict management strategies (Collaboration)	Does not use appropriate conflict management strategies.	Attempts to use conflict management strategies but gets defensive and/or does not listen to peer feedback.	Uses conflict management strategies without getting defensive. Writes down peer feedback in design notebook.	Uses conflict management strategies without getting defensive. Uses peer feedback to improve solution or idea.
Use of appropriate tools	Does not use available tools or is not able to explain why a tool is appropriate to use.	Chooses appropriate tools to use but is not able to fully explain why the tools are appropriate for the task.	Chooses appropriate tools to use and fully explains why the tools are appropriate for the task.	Chooses the appropriate tools to use and fully explains why the tools aid in efficiency and effectiveness for the task. Suggests additional tools that might have been even more helpful to use or try.

(Continued)

(Continued)

ISP 2 COMPONENTS	NEEDS MORE SUPPORT	APPROACHES EXPECTATION	MEETS EXPECTATION	ACHIEVING SOCIETAL CHANGE AGENT
Iterative design	Does not engage in multiple trials of the solution. Provides ideas or solutions but does not test them.	Provides ideas or solutions and completes one test. Does not use the results to improve the solution.	Provides ideas or solutions and completes at least two tests. Uses the results to improve the solution before testing another time.	Provides ideas or solutions and completes multiple iterations of testing until the goal is achieved for the task. Results are used to improve the solution each time.
Design notebook	Has a design notebook, but does not use it for recording ideas, feedback, test results, and final results.	Has a design notebook and records some of the ideas, feedback, and test results. Missing pieces to the iterative process.	Has a design notebook that has a running record of ideas, solutions, feedback, test results, change ideas, and final results.	Has a design notebook that has a running record of ideas, solutions, feedback, test results, change ideas, and final results. There are sketches, clear connection of change ideas to test results, and ideas for future solutions based on the final result.

Stop, Think, Reflect (3C)

1. How could you use ISP 2 in your own classroom?

2. How could you turn a current lesson into one that engages scholars with ISP 2?

 Available for download at **qrs.ly/s9f1lux**

 **Recap This!**

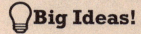**Big Ideas!**

ISP 2

Collaborate and Use Appropriate Tools to Engage in Iterative Design

The most meaningful STEM tasks are deeply interwoven with scholars' lives and interests. Intentional **collaboration** builds collective ownership in seeking solutions to big and messy topics we encounter in our world. Engaging in ISP 2 provides scholars a collaborative outlet to hone their iterative design and solution-seeking skills.	**Using appropriate tools** for solution seeking in STEM happens best when our scholars are able to collaborate and build off each other's ideas, thoughts, and strategies. When the voices of scholars are heard, they can collaborate with multiple and diverse ideas. Scholars have the opportunity to make sense of their ideas and work toward creating a plan that would allow them to gather evidence to draw conclusions.
Iterative solution seeking is essential so scholars experience firsthand to not accept ideas at face value. Through this iterative process, scholars collaborate to plan, test, draw conclusions, refine, retest, and draw new conclusions. Collaborating helps scholars to see the world from viewpoints outside their own lived experiences and is generative toward building a sense of urgency scholars need to be advocates and change-makers in service of a more equitable and just world.	Don't wait to engage your scholars in ISP 2! Frequent experiences to **iteratively seek solutions** through design and experimentation with appropriate tools is an essential collaborative process for scholars and is essential to foster STEM content, practices, and skills.

●●● STEM STARTERS

- Resist the urge to overguide your scholars. When scholars engage in iterative planning, testing, refining, and retesting, it is tempting to provide more guidance than needed. However, you want your scholars to do the thinking and navigating through the task. If they get too frustrated, it becomes unproductive. Ask probing questions to redirect or suggest a new tool they can try, but don't do the thinking for them! Although they might be relieved in the moment, if you "tell" them what to do, you are really depriving them of the thinking opportunity and acquisition of knowledge and understanding.

- Using appropriate tools isn't about telling scholars what tools to use. As a STEM educator, it's your job to have many possible tools accessible to scholars, but it should be up to them to decide when and how to use them.

- Tools don't have to be expensive; they can be no- or low-cost items.

- Adopting an ISP mindset can help you organize how to integrate STEM practices and content across different STEM disciplines seamlessly, which can lead to more effective and meaningful learning experiences for your scholars!

- Keeping access and equity considerations at the forefront of ISP tasks is a commitment to more meaningful, contextual, and empathy-driven STEM learning experiences for all scholars! ●

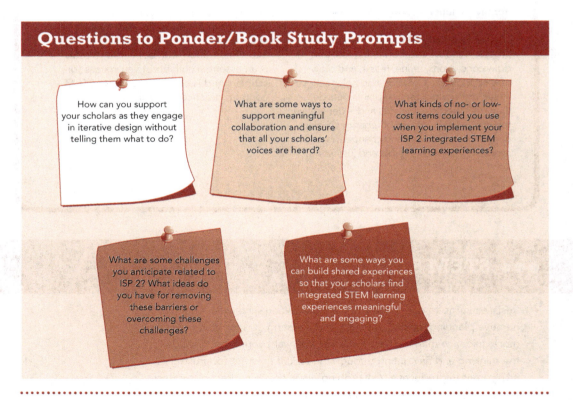

Questions to Ponder/Book Study Prompts

How can you support your scholars as they engage in iterative design without telling them what to do?

What are some ways to support meaningful collaboration and ensure that all your scholars' voices are heard?

What kinds of no- or low-cost items could you use when you implement your ISP 2 integrated STEM learning experiences?

What are some challenges you anticipate related to ISP 2? What ideas do you have for removing these barriers or overcoming these challenges?

What are some ways you can build shared experiences so that your scholars find integrated STEM learning experiences meaningful and engaging?

online resources

Available for download at **qrs.ly/s9f1lux**

TRY THIS!

Whether you're trying a new STEM task or reimagining one you've used in the past, try the following in Table 3.3 to highlight the aspects of ISP 2 we have discussed in this chapter.

Table 3.3

ISP 2: Collaborate and Use Appropriate Tools to Engage in Iterative Design

COMPONENTS TO ISP 2	ASPECTS OF TASK	QUESTION PROMPTS FOR SCHOLARS
Collaboration	Clearly defined roles	How did your role contribute to the group's success? How did the other roles contribute to the group's success?
	Need for multiple perspectives	How would your solution have been different if you did this task alone? Do you think working with others led to a better solution?
	Sense of belonging	How were your ideas valued in your group? How did your team support one another to meet the criteria of this task?
Use of appropriate tools	Availability of materials	How did the availability of materials impact your group's design?
	Rationale for materials	Why did you choose the materials you used in your project?
	Trade-offs with materials	Why did you not choose other materials? What materials would you have liked to use but were not available?
Iterative design	Isolate one variable	Why did you choose to focus on this variable instead of another? How does focusing on this piece help you meet the criteria?
	Improve model	What changes did you make to your design? What hypothesis can you make about the impact this change will have?
	Retest and collect data	What data did you collect in your new test? Based on your data, did your design changes improve your model?

CHAPTER 4

ISP 3: COMMUNICATE SOLUTIONS BASED ON EVIDENCE AND DATA

In the following story, you will meet Mrs. Muncy, a third-grade teacher who engages her scholars in the ISP of communicating solutions based on evidence and data. As you read, look for . . .

- How Mrs. Muncy facilitates scholars' communication of solutions based on evidence and data

- How scholars use evidence and data to communicate solutions

- Ways the learning experience provides opportunities for scholars to collect data and use evidence to communicate solutions

●●● THE STORY OF MRS. MUNCY

Mrs. Muncy (she/her) was exhausted from the weekend. Her town had been recovering from floods that resulted from a deluge of rain that came after a long drought in the area. Mrs. Muncy's church had been assembling and distributing supplies to area residents, some of whom were families of the scholars in her third-grade class. As she prepared to teach an Earth Science unit, she hadn't anticipated how relevant the unit on natural hazards would be. In the past, when Mrs. Muncy taught about *natural hazards and how humans can reduce their impacts*, she usually brought in a real-life example of a historic flood that had happened years ago in a neighboring county. Making connections between her scholars' lives and the local area was something Mrs. Muncy wanted to do when she planned a unit. She was always keeping her eyes open for opportunities to connect the classroom experience with news the scholars or elders in the community might know about. Now more than ever, scholars understood firsthand the devastating effects of flooding, and their desire to help the community was palpable. Many of her scholars were facing food insecurity and housing instability since the flood, and they were understandably distracted in class because of this natural disaster. Mrs. Muncy hoped that refocusing the context of this lesson on the recent events might help scholars engage in class, help them understand why the floods had been so fast and so pronounced, and what members of the community were trying to do to protect the area from further damage.

Mrs. Muncy began the inquiry by taking the scholars outside to observe the schoolyard and record signs of flooding near the school. The scholars quickly noticed sandbags that had been placed around the school's entrance a few weeks earlier. At first, scholars focused only on the recent preparations that had been added to the school when folks knew the rains were coming and had tried to prevent damage. To encourage deeper thinking, Mrs. Muncy asked them to look at the original design of the landscape, building, and parking lots that existed before the flood. Yvette mentioned that the wall she was standing on was probably meant to be a flood barrier when the school was built. Rashad noticed different surfaces of the pavement—some areas were concrete while others were rocky or had soil. There were parts of the schoolyard that had vegetation and trees, and scholars noticed that the soil lines that were still evident from where the water level had risen didn't come up as high to the school building as in areas where there was only concrete. Mrs. Muncy told scholars to capture these elements as they drew a picture of the school in their design notebooks. She then had scholars measure off a square meter where they stood and estimated the amount of vegetation in their square. By creating a grid in their design notebook, scholars were able to represent the vegetation for their area as a fraction, where the numerator consisted of the fraction of plants in the square meter and the denominator was 100. Once scholars created a fraction, they had to make a claim about how fast or slow water moved within their specific grid. For example, Jason's fraction had zero in the numerator because his square meter was completely concrete. He claimed water would move fast within his grid because it was concrete pavement with no plants to slow the water. Rochelle noticed her plot had soil, but it was so packed down that it felt as hard as the concrete. This provided scholars with an experience to notice the impact of human activities on natural hazards, specifically how humans planned the schoolyard and the impact of that planning on flood control.

Back in the classroom, Mrs. Muncy talked to scholars about weather patterns. Specifically, their area within the United States was experiencing El Niño, a cyclical weather pattern that brings increased rainfall that increases the risk of flooding. Mrs. Muncy asked a meteorologist to visit the class virtually to describe how she forecasts the weather using mathematical modeling. Having the meteorologist come to class gave scholars a chance to ask questions about how accurate forecasting is and what kinds of technology are used to make these predictions.

Because scientists monitor and track these patterns, humans can plan for the impact of weather events. The floodwall on the other side of town was one way their town had worked to reduce the impacts of flooding. Mrs. Muncy had scholars investigate other ways their local government had acted to reduce the impacts of the predictable increased rainfall during El Niño. Clayton found a newspaper article explaining how the city added storm drains in his neighborhood. The storm drains led into concrete ditches that fed into a stream near the baseball practice fields that were still underwater. Mrs. Muncy asked the class to model the effectiveness of the flood controls in their town. (See Figure 4.1.)

Scholars noticed the flood controls worked well for part of town, but for the part of town where their school was located, there were fewer projects to help with flood control. In fact, as Clayton's research showed, some areas in his neighborhood were collecting the excess water. "I wonder why some areas of town have better ways to prevent flooding than others," Maya asked. Mrs. Muncy picked up on Maya's observation and began a discussion about evaluating the design solutions they researched. Scholars made a list of the design solutions they had investigated, including the flood wall, extra storm drains, and sandbags that were around their school. Mrs. Muncy provided scholars with materials to create prototypes of the design solutions and then test how they reduced the impact of flooding caused by excessive rainfall. Mrs. Muncy also made a note to later revisit the idea of flood plains and inequities that often exist around housing in flood-prone areas.

The scholars were excited the day Mrs. Muncy had them test their prototypes. Each group had made a different prototype. Maya's group had a solid wall made out of clay to model the floodwall. Liam's group used small bags filled with sand to model the sandbags around the school. Clayton's group used straws of different diameters to model storm drains to see the extent to which increasing the speed of water draining decreased the chances of flooding. The goal was to see which model reduced the impact of the flood best. The flood would be simulated by pouring a controlled amount of water into the container in which scholars had built their models. Mrs. Muncy led a conversation with scholars to determine criteria for success. "Obviously less water is better," Clayton suggested.

"But how do we measure that?" Mrs. Muncy inquired. After further discussion, scholars agreed that success for flood control would be

Figure 4.1

Scholars Test Their Models to Determine Which Materials Are Most Effective for Controlling the Flow of Water

Source: Tracy Young

based on not having standing water in protected places for more than 5 seconds. With the criteria defined, each scholar took a role in their group as the recorder, the timer, or the water pourer, and all took part in constructing the model and recording and analyzing data in their design notebook. Based on their group data, scholars created a claim, evidence, and reasoning chart to capture their ideas about the best flood controls for their town. (See Figure 4.2.)

Figure 4.2

Claim, Evidence, Reasoning Chart

Scientific Question:_____

Claim: What do you know about the question? Write a simple statement or answer the question above.

Evidence: How do you know what you know? Use data or evidence to prove your claim.

Reasoning: How does your evidence support your claim? What did you learn?

 Available for download at **qrs.ly/s9f1lux**

They were required to be specific about the STEM content applied to help them arrive at their solutions. A whole class discussion brought all the group information together on the final day of experiments.

Mrs. Muncy wanted scholars to share what they had learned with others for the final assessment. Scholars wanted to talk to others about their ideas on what could be done around the school and beyond to minimize the chance of the floods causing destruction in the future. The principal, facilities team, and city council representatives were invited to the classroom presentations where scholars shared their ideas. Using their data, sketches of the schoolyard, and claims, evidence, and reasoning charts, scholars offered ideas such as increasing drainage and building small floodwalls to reduce the impact of flooding in their neighborhood. The principal was pleased to see that scholars wanted to get involved in making these changes happen around their school. The scholars came away from this unit ready to spearhead the creation of action plans to improve the schools' ability to handle future floods and with an overall feeling of being able to contribute to the challenges that faced their community. ●

Source: From Cook & Bush, 2015.

●●● SO YOU'VE BEEN TOLD . . .

Mathematical modeling is about using physical or virtual manipulatives in mathematics instruction.

REALITY CHECK!

Mathematical modeling is not synonymous with using manipulatives to make sense of mathematics. Sometimes when we use manipulatives (physical or virtual) or tools, we do use models or representations to build our understanding of mathematics, but mathematical modeling is really a process and is often well revealed and actualized in very contextual, messy scenarios (Consortium for Mathematics and Its Applications [COMAP] & Society for Industrial and Applied Mathematics [SIAM], 2019). In the story of Mrs. Muncy, real historical data and trends were analyzed to make predictions for the next decade. This information involved numerous data points, not all perfectly aligned (just as when you see multiple weather models on TV that are attempting to predict the path of a hurricane). What will ultimately happen is still uncertain, but best-educated forecasts can be made from data that do exist as well as other known variables. Meaningful experiences with mathematical modeling don't just happen by chance. Engaging scholars deeply in authentic ISP tasks provides a pathway for practice and experiences with both mathematical modeling as well as representing or using models to understand mathematics. ●

Planning STEM learning experiences around current events is a ton of work.

REALITY CHECK!

Not true. Planning STEM learning experiences around current events necessitates a flexible mindset and can be a little unpredictable, but what better way to mirror how life actually works! In our everyday professional and personal lives, we daily encounter unpredictable (and predictable) issues and challenges. Being flexible, in-the-moment, and having the ability to pivot and prioritize are key life skills that scholars will carry with them for a lifetime. You, as their teacher, modeling a curious and calm presence in the face of uncertainty is a meaningful gift you can't afford not to give to your scholars! **•**

What Is ISP 3: Communicate Solutions Based on Evidence and Data

Communication is a critical employability skill that is one of the most cited among industry, business, and nonprofit communities. While communication is a critical societal skill, ISP 3 goes beyond the social idea of communication and focuses more on *how* to communicate various solutions and ideas using key evidence and data to solve problems, especially messy, wicked intractable problems. Across all the SEPs, SMPs, and TEPs, scholars are asked to make choices about *how* to effectively communicate their solutions or ideas. Communication can look different in a variety of contexts, and scholars are encouraged to be creative and use multiple modes of communication to share their solutions and ideas.

While much of communication often focuses on multiple modalities in order to present ideas and solutions, it's first important to consider what evidence and data you might have.

- Do your data and evidence answer your initial questions?

- Do your data and evidence include representative voices? What voices might be missing from your evidence or data?

- Do your data and evidence provide space for multiple scenarios to communicate and talk through?

Communicating solutions based on evidence and data means *listening, discussing,* and *defending* (Bostic et al., 2019). Are your data and evidence strong enough to stand behind to communicate or do you need to collect more? (See Figure 4.3.)

Figure 4.3

Scholars Collect Data to See Which Materials Hold up When Exposed to Extended Sunlight

Source: Tracy Young

A key feature in communicating solutions based on evidence and data is to focus on objectivity—elevating the truth of the data and evidence. This can sometimes be challenging for scholars in a world filled with social media, untruths, and other images or communication styles that don't always lend themselves to the truth. Further, scholars will want to insert their own opinions or interpretations that may include bias or untruth. Focusing on the following questions can help scholars consider if what they are about to communicate is objective:

- What does your evidence or data tell you about your idea or solution?

- How would you describe your solution without using the words "I think," "I like," or "I feel"?

- Who or what does your solution(s) or idea(s) impact? Who or what might be negatively impacted by your solution(s) or idea(s)?

After taking into consideration the quality and objectivity of the evidence and data, scholars should collaborate to create a communication plan and execute it. It is important to consider multiple audiences when considering the communication plan. It is also key, especially when scholars are collaborating together with various backgrounds and expertise, to facilitate an environment where scholars can listen to each other, use various representations in the communications, and coherently communicate the solutions or ideas. Within this collaboration is the heart of this ISP—scholars have the opportunity to work together within this social context, learning and listening to each other and, from their data and evidence, developing a deeper understanding of the content and the ability to work in teams.

Finally, encouraging scholars, within their collaborations, to embrace new and different ways of presenting ideas and solutions is important. The most critical question to answer is—Who is our audience and what would best speak to them? It is important to consider our audience outside the traditional realm and be inclusive of the nontraditional, which lies outside traditional values and the general way we do things. This could be an oral presentation with rich illustrations; an idea book filled with sketches and illustrations; 3D printed, 3D pen creation, and other types of created models of various solutions, short media clips or videos, photographs, and so on. We discourage the heavy use of paragraphs and words unless absolutely necessary. Asking scholars to write long paragraphs after having them engage in a hands-on creative process can directly counteract how we define progress and quality. Ultimately, scholars should be given the space and time to evaluate and look at their data and evidence, refine them as necessary, share their ideas and strategies within their collaborative group to create a plan to communicate their solutions and ideas, and then share their solutions and ideas using a variety of meaningful methods that lift the objectivity and voices in their data and evidence.

Available for download at **qrs.ly/s9f1lux**

Why Does ISP 3 Matter?

What is communication? What does effective communication look like in the classroom and outside the school walls? Let's take a moment to consider a scenario on communication outside the realm of the classroom. Imagine having the knowledge, skills, and wherewithal to end all hunger, strife, and bitterness that exist in the world. We would have a more just society. We could live with less worry and anger—resulting in better health. Positive life-changing effects would exist for all. You contemplate ways to communicate your thoughts with others. You are invited to meet with eight other like-minded individuals to share and discuss ideas. At the meeting, as you share your thoughts and ideas, the group intensely listens. You continue to speak. They listen. They speak. But you fail to listen to their strategies. Instead, you sit rehearsing what you are going to say next. Another individual stands up and offers an alternative solution to end hunger, strife, and bitterness using charts and models. The group interacts and continues to listen intently. You, on the other hand, sit in your seat, ruffle through some papers, and respond to emails. When the individual concludes their remarks, you stand up and begin speaking, picking up where *you* left off—not connecting your conversation to any of the strategies shared. You look at everyone in the room and wrap up saying, "And that's what we need to do to bring about change." Satisfied, you smile at everyone, nod your head as a form of thank you, pack up your things, and leave. You are confident in what you communicated to the group, and you know you left the group with a stellar plan.

Meanwhile, the group continues discussing and critiquing each other's plans and strategies. As each plan is revisited and more information is gathered and discussed, the group offers constructive criticism and feedback. It is through this collaboration and communication that the group is able to develop a deeper understanding of the underlying influences of hunger, strife, and bitterness. They collectively work to design a plan based on all the evidence and data they heard from each member of the group. Satisfied, they use formulas, graphs, and models to communicate their solutions that would result in a decline of hunger, strife, and bitterness that exists in the world.

Weeks later, you return to the group expecting a congratulatory praise but are mystified you do not receive any. You are flabbergasted that the solutions the group implemented are not ones you had shared. How did they bring about change without using your design? You sit and reflect on what you shared with the group. What you shared was viable. However, there were some concerns with your solutions that the group tried to point out. You refused to listen and continued speaking. The group was listening to your explanations and solution strategies, but you were not listening to theirs.

Communication involves more than verbal speaking. It involves active listening from both the person who is speaking and those being spoken to. See Figure 4.4.

We cannot bring about any positive change without communication grounded in data and evidence and a variety of different perspectives.

Figure 4.4

One Scholar Shares Their Design Idea While Another Scholar Actively Listens

Source: Julie Sicks-Panus

When we provide space for our scholars to communicate and collaborate, they are empowered. Their voice matters and makes a difference. As they communicate their solutions, they see and hear the strengths and weaknesses in not only others' solutions but theirs as well. Why is this important? It is important because we want our scholars to justify and explain their solutions with evidence. We do not want to ill-equip our scholars with ill-defined solutions and have them rely on empty words or justifications when making solutions. If we do, we would be living in a quicksand society where we would sink with every step because of lack of evidence and time to see the holes in our solutions. As Dr. Talithia Williams exclaims, "Show me the Data!" Scholars have the opportunity to reason and make sense of their and their peers' explanations and communicate their solutions using representations such as models, tables, graphs, or other figures.

Stop, Think, Reflect (4B)

1. How did you see Mrs. Muncy engage young scholars in ISP 3? What specific actions did she use throughout the task?

2. How did scholars collect data throughout the task?

3. How were scholars supported in making and justifying claims in the task?

4. In what ways were scholars expected to communicate the effectiveness of their solutions?

 Available for download at **qrs.ly/s9f1lux**

Diving Deeper: Mrs. Muncy as a STEM System Disruptor

In the Controlling the Floods task, scholars had an immediate context presented in their community with the recent flooding. In this learning experience, Mrs. Muncy challenged the STEM status quo ideas of objectivity and one right way. Because the challenge used the context of recent town flooding, empathy was critical. Beyond data and logical facts, the thoughts of others had to be taken into account, such as why one area of town had more flood damage than other areas. Mrs. Muncy also challenged the idea that there was only one right way to complete something. Scholars had multiple designs to address flood control and shared those diverse ideas with others.

Mrs. Muncy drew upon the context of floods because she knew it was at the top of everyone's minds and would be likely to engage scholars in authentic "need-to-knows." Even without a context such as this to readily draw upon, Mrs. Muncy used the local town history as the context to study the same STEM concepts in previous years. Centering STEM curricula in relevant contexts is important to engaging learners in the science they see around them. Doing this helps connect scholars to their "funds of knowledge" (Moll et al., 1992) or the skills and

 knowledge that have been developed historically and culturally within their communities. Because each place is rooted in a unique and important context, this place-based approach to inquiry helps to connect learners to what they are learning. It provides an opportunity for scholars to **empathize** with others related to their STEM instruction.

Scholars learn that what they are doing in class relates to and has an impact on their community. Most scholars naturally want to help others, so empathy can be used to engage them in inquiry and sustain their interest when they know what they are learning will benefit others (Bush & Cook, 2019; Bush et al., 2022).

Extending from the focus on empathy, STEM learning can be a powerful experience when connected to helping others. In this lesson, Mrs. Muncy built in the culminating experience to include scholars having the opportunity to share what they learned with the principal, facilities team, and city council representatives at the school. This opportunity included scholars making recommendations based on data, where they had the opportunity to describe how different designs led to less flooding because of faster water drainage or determent. Their discussions even led to

 plans for action such as teacher-led grants and fundraising projects to make some of the scholars' ideas on how to prevent or minimize flooding near the school a reality. The STEM lesson became an **empowering** experience for scholars—an important feeling for them to have especially in light of the recent events of the flood being out of their control.

Teachers can emphasize and highlight the amazing things humans have done over time to minimize weather-related disasters and develop systems to predict future events. This helps illuminate how scholars, through their STEM learning experiences, can be part of the solution and even come up with novel ways to help others and their communities—and helps scholars feel more self-agency in an otherwise bewildering situation. As scholars empathize with those who have been affected  by the various STEM-related issues they are studying and become empowered to help contribute and iteratively seek solutions, they are developing their STEM identity. **STEM identity development** enables scholars to see themselves in STEM and to have a sense of belonging within STEM.

This is important even if scholars decide not to go into a STEM-related career. Regardless of their chosen path, it is important for all members of society to understand the conversations surrounding them that invoke STEM content and practices and to know they have an important voice in those conversations. As scholars became knowledgeable about flood mitigation and land use trends in their area, for example, they came to see themselves as people who could offer ideas and solutions to others.

Putting ISP 3 Into Action: What Does It Look Like?

Scholars communicate to gather information needed to solve a problem, share ideas and strategies to create a plan, and share solutions using effective presentations. In Table 4.1, we describe what engagement in ISP 3 would look like in the classroom.

Table 4.1

Putting ISP 3 Into Action

	ISP 3 COMPONENTS	TEACHER ACTIONS	SCHOLAR ACTIONS
ISP 3: Communicate solutions based on evidence and data	Gathering data and evidence	Provide opportunities to practice gathering data. Help scholars identify and/or create measurable criteria for success.	Practice gathering data from multiple sources. Identify or create ways to measure success.

(Continued)

	ISP 3 COMPONENTS	TEACHER ACTIONS	SCHOLAR ACTIONS
ISP 3: Communicate solutions based on evidence and data (continued)	Gathering data and evidence (continued)	Encourage data collection that captures multiple voices and perspectives. Include types data needed to provide solutions or new ideas.	Identify or create ways to measure success (continued). Ensure types of data capture all voices.
	Creating a data or evidence plan	Offer opportunities for scholars to create and test prototypes of design solutions. Share different ways to organize data with scholars. Offer a tool (e.g., claim, evidence, reasoning) or other representations for creating evidence-based ideas or solutions. Provide space to learn and practice multiple communication technologies and methods.	Plan, make/create, and test design solutions. Make intentional decisions about how to organize and display data. Use a model(s) or other various representations and tools such as claim, evidence, and reasoning to create evidence-based ideas or solutions. Create a communication plan to share ideas and strategies toward the solution(s).
	Communicating the solutions or ideas to stakeholders	Allow scholars the space and opportunity to present solutions or ideas in a variety of formats to a stakeholder audience. Ensure listening, particularly to perspectives different from your own, is seen as an essential component of communicating. Create space and opportunity for scholars to listen, critique, debate, and provide meaningful feedback in order to continue to refine solutions and ideas.	Communicate solutions or ideas using a variety of representations that elevate the voices objectively within the data and evidence to stakeholder audiences. Listen, embrace, reason, and defend, if necessary, feedback from peers and stakeholders on solutions and ideas in order to continue to refine them.

Integrated STEM is primarily science.

REALITY CHECK!

Not true. In integrated STEM tasks, the *context* is often science focused. But technology, engineering, and mathematics are all essential and front-and-center in integrated STEM. Advances in technology enable the field to push forward in ways that were not historically possible, such as the ability to communicate and seek solutions across continents, synthesize incredible amounts of information quickly, and, in the story of Mrs. Muncy, the opportunity to engage in messy models of mathematics. Engineering empowers scholars to develop, create, and build toward the solutions they are seeking—and sometimes this component ends up being front and center. Finally, mathematics is the vehicle through which we interpret and make sense of science and is the gateway to STEM, not the gatekeeper (National Science and Technology Council, 2018). ●

Assessing ISP 3

Mrs. Muncy assessed ISP 3 with scholars' artifacts of learning. For example, sketching is an important way to represent thinking and to participate in brainstorming, planning, and communicating solutions (Kelley & Sung, 2017). In this learning experience, scholars drew pictures to record observational data and recorded their data from testing their prototypes in their design notebooks. Scholars also used claims, evidence, and reasoning charts in their design notebooks as a way to demonstrate their claims were based on evidence. These artifacts focused on the process of doing ISP 3 where scholars could practice gathering data and formulating claims.

Mrs. Muncy also assessed how scholars applied their knowledge as they communicated their solutions. Instead of a written report or class presentation, Mrs. Muncy empowered scholars to share their learning with decision makers. When scholars presented their ideas to the principal, facilities teams, and city council representatives, they used the data they had gathered to share their findings. The scholars' presentations included recommendations for future flood control with specific action steps based on the data from their investigations. This provided not only another real-world connection for scholars using their STEM content knowledge but also a meaningful way for Mrs. Muncy to assess how scholars were able to apply their content knowledge to real-world settings.

In the Moment Feedback

In the Moment Feedback is a tool that educators can use as they assess scholars on ISP 3. The first set of questions are formative assessment questions meant to generate a discussion among and between you and your scholars. Such discussions will help you gain an understanding of where scholars are and what additional supports they might need as they engage in ISP 3. The Design Notebook Prompts are prompts you can provide your scholars for them to respond in writing to facilitate literacy and written communication, encourage engineering design thinking processes, and serve as a record of activity similar to what is often expected in the workforce. We encourage the use of the design notebook that showcases scholars' growth on ISP 3.

Formative Assessment Questions (teachers asking scholars)

Purpose: In the Moment Feedback

- What is the most compelling piece of evidence supporting your proposed solution?

- What pieces of evidence demonstrate the effectiveness of your solution?

- If you were to describe your solution in 1 minute or less, what would you say?

- What is the "so what" of your solution? Why does your solution matter?

- Who or what does your solution negatively impact? What are you doing to address that?

- How did you determine what success was for this learning experience?

Design Notebook Prompts (scholars complete individually or in groups)

Purpose: Continuous record of learning experiences/final showcase of work

- The most compelling piece of evidence we have that supports our proposed solution is _____. Because . . . (explain why).

- We minimized our personal feelings in our analysis by _____. (addressing bias)

- The top three takeaways for our proposed solution for stakeholders are _____.

- If we were to draw the impact of our proposed solution, it would look like <draw or write>.

- If we were to hold a debate for our proposed solution, the two sides would be _____ and _____. Two facts on each side are . . .

- If we were to design an infographic on one piece of data for the proposed solution, it would look like <draw or insert infographic>.

  Available for download at **qrs.ly/s9f1lux**

ISP 3 RUBRIC

In Table 4.2 we provide a rubric that you can use to assess your scholars' engagement in ISP 3.

Table 4.2

ISP 3 Rubric

ISP 3 COMPONENTS	NEEDS MORE SUPPORT	APPROACHES EXPECTATION	MEETS EXPECTATION	ACHIEVING SOCIETAL CHANGE AGENT
Gathering data or evidence	Data or evidence are not collected or only one type of data is collected. It is unclear how the data or evidence were collected.	Multiple data or evidence are collected. It is somewhat unclear how the data or evidence were collected. Data and evidence are disorganized. Some stakeholder voices were left out.	Describes and articulates how multiple data or evidence are collected. Data or evidence are organized in such a way to be able to look at and draw conclusions. Stakeholders' voices are included throughout.	Describes and articulates multiple data or evidence collected with justifications. Data and evidence are organized to look at and draw conclusions. Whose voice might be left out of the stakeholders was considered and then captured in the data and evidence.
Creating a data or evidence plan	Data or evidence being collected are not clear. No research has been completed that might have pointed to solutions or ideas. It is unclear what the goal or what success looks like for the solution or idea.	Data or evidence plan is vaguely defined. Some research has been conducted. It is unclear if the stakeholders were considered in the plan.	Data or evidence plan is clearly defined. Variables have been considered. Research of potential ideas or solutions is evident. Stakeholders are considered in the plan.	Data or evidence plan is specifically defined as well as the constraints or variables. Multiple data or evidence are considered. All stakeholders are included in the plan with a rationale.

(Continued)

(Continued)

ISP 3 COMPONENTS	NEEDS MORE SUPPORT	APPROACHES EXPECTATION	MEETS EXPECTATION	ACHIEVING SOCIETAL CHANGE AGENT
Communicating* the solutions or ideas to stakeholders *Communication can mean oral, written, mixed media, video, or other form of communication that serves to tell the story.	Communication of the solution or idea does not yet include data or evidence.	Communication is organized and present but does not yet objectively showcase data or evidence used for creating solutions or ideas. It is unclear the impact on the stakeholders.	Communication is organized and presents multiple representations to the different possible solutions or ideas, what tests or trials or models were completed, the results, and reflection. Impact on stakeholders is present throughout.	Communication is organized and presents a clear story of the idea or solution. Solutions and ideas are objectively presented and feedback is listened to and rebutted (if necessary). It elevates the voices of all stakeholders, including the impact on them. It offers recommendations for future iterations of the solutions or ideas and possible models that might predict outcomes.

Stop, Think, Reflect (4C)

1. How could you use ISP 3 in your own classroom?

2. How could you turn a current lesson into one that engages scholars with ISP 3?

 Available for download at **qrs.ly/s9f1lux**

 **Recap This!**

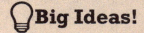**Big Ideas!**

ISP 3

Communicate Solutions Based on Evidence and Data

ISP 3 positions scholars to **communicate** to gather information needed to solve a challenge, share ideas and strategies to create a plan, and share solutions using effective presentations.	Science should not be driven by opinions. When scholars engage in ISP 3, their solution seeking is **driven by evidence and data**, such as through conducting tests and trials, reviewing research, using representations, and analyzing mathematical models and data.
As scholars **communicate solutions**, they should be prepared to justify their recommendations, predictions, and forecasts on evidence and data.	**Communication** is an iterative and cyclical process. Scholars communicate as they work to gather evidence and data. Scholars communicate as they analyze evidence and data. Scholars communicate as they revise and refine their thinking. As scholars communicate final recommendations based on evidence and data, they might encounter new ways of thinking that cause them to reconsider and reenter the cycle.

●●● STEM STARTERS

- Embrace the unpredictable and messiness. The most meaningful STEM tasks often originate from current events and scholar interests. This can be unpredictable as it is unknown what will happen next or be the ultimate outcome. It can also be messy because as teachers, we don't know all the answers. Just remember, this is important for your scholars to see you embrace, as this can help them to emulate and believe that they too can embrace unpredictable, multifaceted, messy situations.

- Authentic situations can be ideal pathways to opportunities for using representations that build understanding and even mathematical modeling. Embrace the conflicting data and multiple predictions and variables. With ISP 3, scholars improve self-efficacy when they navigate choppy waters and weigh different considerations to arrive at an ultimate proposed solution or recommendation.

- Leverage the needs and interests of the community! In the story of Mrs. Muncy, the community was in crisis. It is often human nature to want to help or contribute in some way during a crisis. By engaging scholars in the Controlling the Floods task, Mrs. Muncy positioned scholars as members of the community who could contribute to ideas and solutions during a time of need. ●

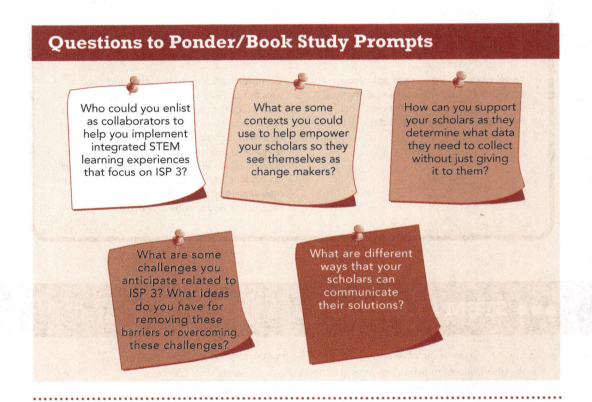

Questions to Ponder/Book Study Prompts

Who could you enlist as collaborators to help you implement integrated STEM learning experiences that focus on ISP 3?

What are some contexts you could use to help empower your scholars so they see themselves as change makers?

How can you support your scholars as they determine what data they need to collect without just giving it to them?

What are some challenges you anticipate related to ISP 3? What ideas do you have for removing these barriers or overcoming these challenges?

What are different ways that your scholars can communicate their solutions?

online resources — Available for download at **qrs.ly/s9f1lux**

TRY THIS!

Whether you're trying a new STEM task or reimagining one you've used in the past, try the following in Table 4.3 to highlight the aspects of ISP 3 we have discussed in this chapter.

Table 4.3

ISP 3: Communicate Solutions Based on Evidence and Data

COMPONENTS TO ISP 3	ASPECTS OF TASK	QUESTION PROMPTS FOR SCHOLARS
Gathering data and evidence	Collecting data and evidence	What is the best way to record and organize your data or evidence? What variables are at play in testing your solution(s) or idea(s)?
	Making observations about the data and evidence	What data or evidence did you collect? What trends are apparent in the evidence or data and how can you use it to improve your design (e.g., iterative design)?
Creating a data or evidence plan	Researching what success looks like	How will you know if your solution or idea is working? What data or evidence will give you feedback on refining the idea or solution? Does success look different for different stakeholders?
	Researching potential solutions	Which solutions did you find to be more effective? Do you think those solutions would be as effective with different criteria? For whom do the solutions work? For whom do the solutions not work? Are there other real-world factors that we cannot simulate in our proposed model (Scholars can understand that models have limits to how realistic they are. This does not negate the value of using a model, but they can understand that models have limits.)?
	Planning, building or creating, and testing a solution	How realistic is your test of the solution? What solutions or ideas do your data and evidence point to? What did you observe that informed your design? Are there multiple ideas or solutions to create and try? When testing your solution or idea, what is your data or evidence revealing to you about its effectiveness or impact?
Communicating the solutions or ideas to stakeholders	Using various representations to objectively present data and evidence	How can you represent the data or evidence using various representations to best communicate findings, ideas, or solutions to stakeholders? How can you use that data or evidence to communicate the effectiveness of your solution?
	Using multiple modes of communications to present ideas or solutions to stakeholders	Whose voices or communities are positively impacted by the ideas and solutions? How are they negatively impacted? How are your ideas or solutions supported objectively with evidence and reasoning?
	Making recommendations for future steps based on their investigation	Is there a representation that can be used with the current data or evidence that would best predict future impact or events? Based on your testing or models, what would you do differently in the future? What resources or additional data or evidence would you want to have to improve the design?

CHAPTER 5

ISP 4: RECOGNIZE AND USE STRUCTURES IN REAL-WORLD SYSTEMS

In the following story, you will meet Mr. Robuson, a first-grade teacher who engages his scholars in the ISP of recognizing and using structures in real-world systems. As you read, look for . . .

- How Mr. Robuson facilitates scholars' recognition and use of real-world systems

- How scholars recognize and use real-world systems

- Ways the learning experience provides opportunities for scholars to recognize and use real-world systems

●●● THE STORY OF MR. ROBUSON

As a kickoff to his unit on how animals and plants have specific parts and characteristics to help them survive, Mr. Robuson (he/him) took his first-grade scholars on a field trip to the local zoo. He recognized having a shared experience would create common background knowledge his scholars could use during the unit. Prior to arriving at the zoo, Mr. Robuson asked his scholars to look for specific parts and characteristics of animals that were unique to the animal and helped them survive in their habitat. He also encouraged field trip chaperones to help scholars identify specific characteristics of animals and habitats as they walked throughout the zoo. As soon as they arrived at the zoo, the scholars excitedly filed off the bus with their notebooks in hand, waiting eagerly. "Hey, look over there! It's a huge turtle on top of the log!" Charlotte beamed.

"Why do you think turtles have those shells?" Mr. Robuson asked.

"For protection," Freddie chimed in.

"Look! A turtle jumped into its shell when another turtle bumped into its back leg!" Chae-Won exclaimed.

Her friend, Aparna, responded, "Maybe it does that when it gets scared."

"Yeah, if I had a shell, I would go in there if I got scared too," Darius said.

Mr. Robuson separated the scholars into their assigned groups with their respective chaperones, and each group went to different exhibits throughout the zoo. The scholars were amazed to see all the different habitats for all the animals. They observed and made sketches of each animal and its habitat in their design notebooks. At the end of the day, the scholars climbed into the bus and couldn't wait to share their sketches with their friends. From the buzz of excitement, Mr. Robuson knew the scholars enjoyed seeing the different animals and their habitats at the zoo.

The next day, Mr. Robuson asked the scholars to take out their design notebooks and share their sketches with their shoulder partner. After they shared, Mr. Robuson had them discuss the function of the different unique characteristics of the animals they observed at the zoo. To begin the discussion, Mr. Robuson held up a picture of an otter and asked why it had thick fur.

"I didn't know otters had fur!" Jackson exclaimed.

"Yes, they have fur. It's not the type of fur we are used to seeing on our cats and dogs, but otters have very thick fur, the thickest fur of any animal. See," Mr. Robuson said, showing the scholars a closeup view of the otter's fur. The class gasped in amazement. "So, why do you think the otter has fur?"

"To help it swim faster."

"To keep it warm."

"Yes, the otter has fur to help keep it insulated and warm. Now, I want you to discuss the function of the unique characteristics of the animals you saw at the zoo." Chae-Won mentioned the turtle's shell protected it from danger. Lexi commented on how the lizard's skin was similar to the colors of the plants where it lived and how that helped it hide. Josh pointed out how he noticed the ducks had webbed feet that helped them swim faster. Devon suggested the color of the rodents he saw helped them hide from snakes and cheetahs.

Hunter shared that the penguins' feathers helped trap the air to keep them warm. Chae-Won and Aparna, who were in Hunter's group, were surprised that the penguin's feathers kept them warm.

Mr. Robuson shared how he heard similarities among many of the scholars who shared characteristics of their animals that provided insulation to help keep them warm. Mr. Robuson showcased some of the scholars' pictures to the whole class and asked scholars to think about what characteristics of each animal would help keep it warm from the cold. He created a t-chart and listed each animal shown in the pictures and included the way the scholars suggested the animals insulated their bodies.

ANIMAL	HOW IT KEEPS WARM
Duck	Feathers
Bear	Fur
Baboon	Fur
Eagle	Feathers
Buffalo	Fur

Mr. Robuson then asked the scholars what kind of insulation they think would be most effective. Darius wondered how the polar bears' fur kept them warm when they got wet. Josh asked if any of the animals changed their insulation when the temperature changed. Mr. Robuson used Josh's question to introduce the concept of biomimicry (e.g., hook and loop tape for burrs, seed spreaders for insects and birds spreading fertilization and pollination), the idea that people can design products and solutions based on unique features of living things. A way to look at adaptations and uniqueness in nature is how these adaptations can be used to find solutions to the world's problems.

Mr. Robuson then shared that scientists just discovered an organism that did not have its own insulation, unlike bears who have fur and penguins who have feathers, and may be in jeopardy of not surviving during the cold winter months. Mr. Robuson challenged the scholars to use biomimicry to design a manufactured insulation system for the organism using the least amount of materials possible. He engaged scholars in a guided exploration of the materials: feathers, cotton balls, aluminum foil, plastic bags, scraps of cloth, and scraps of cardboard. In the guided exploration, Mr. Robuson asked scholars to describe the properties of each material. What was heavy? What was light? What was bendable? What was rigid? In what circumstances would these properties be useful to provide an insulation system? How could there be multiple forms of insulation working together in an insulation system? He

Figure 5.1

A Scholar Tests Different Materials to Determine Which Materials Are More Effective Insulators

Source: Tracy Young

encouraged scholars to use their experience at the zoo, their examination of the photos and the t-chart, and their exploration of materials as inspiration to brainstorm ideas for their systems. See Figure 5.1.

The next day Mr. Robuson began class by asking scholars to share the ideas they brainstormed and how they were inspired by structures from nature. Josh shared that he would fill plastic bags with cotton balls and tape the bags together so that the organism could crawl into to keep warm, similar to how he saw the animals huddling together at the zoo. Chae-Won shared, "One idea I had was to cover cardboard with aluminum foil because aluminum foil keeps food warm." After some of the scholars shared, Mr. Robuson placed scholars in groups and asked each group to agree on an idea and create a plan for an insulation system.

Aparna and Darius agreed to use plastic bags, cotton balls, and scraps of cloth to create their design. "Tell me how your idea was inspired by something in nature," Mr. Robuson asked.

"Well, we're trying to mimic the penguin and the seals. We are going to stuff cotton balls into the plastic bags to make a barrier, like seals' blubber. Then we're going to use the cloth scraps as an outside layer to help catch air like the penguins."

The scholars spent the next few days working on creating and testing models of their insulation systems. They used scientific knowledge they gained at the zoo to think about how animals have different forms of insulation. The scholars tracked data on a whiteboard about how much materials they used so they could improve the efficiency of their models. Efficiency could include cost, ease of manufacturing, materials, and so on. It's important to consider, when talking about efficiency, that more is not always better. Mr. Robuson gave scholars thermometers to measure the temperature "inside" of the insulation to determine if the system worked to keep the organism warm. The scholars then recorded the temperatures on the whiteboard alongside the amounts of materials used. After scholars had the chance to test and improve their models at least twice, Mr. Robuson asked his scholars to look at their whiteboards and their data and decide what worked best and make a statement about what materials or parts they thought were important in the insulation system. Mr. Robuson recorded their recommendations on the board.

Mr. Robuson then announced that the school's annual coat and glove drive was coming up and reminded scholars that it gets really cold in the winter. He asked, "What recommendations could we share with people who want to donate a coat or gloves?" The scholars brainstormed ideas. It was important that any recommendations be helpful and not limit the donor's options of coats and gloves.

Josh shared, "It is important to have multiple parts working together, like a zipper and a lot of materials to keep the wind out."

"It's important that there are no holes in the gloves, and they cover your whole hand," Darius added.

"I like how you focused on the different pieces working together in a system. That kind of information will be helpful to people thinking about donating items," Mr. Robuson said. Mr. Robuson wanted scholars to know they had a role in helping—both individually and collectively. After coming up with a list of recommendations for donations (such as food, shoes, shirts, jeans, shorts), including having multiple ways to insulate and make the best use of materials, Mr. Robuson helped scholars create posters using specific phrases to hang near the collection bins. Further, Mr. Robuson helped scholars set a goal for the donation and talked through why it is their goal. He loved watching his scholars take hold of ideas like this to connect STEM with their daily lives and come up with creative ideas to educate others. ●

●●● SO YOU'VE BEEN TOLD . . .

Leave society's biggest challenges to the experts. Only those qualified need to know and learn about really deep and specific problems in society. Most of my scholars will never need to know this.

REALITY CHECK!

This thinking is problematic for several reasons. First, it continues to perpetuate lack of access. We don't know what we don't know. If we do not expose scholars to learning opportunities (in a developmentally appropriate way), they won't be informed personally about the world and professionally they won't be aware of specific careers that exist or potential ways to make contributions to the world. Second, those historically "at the table" making decisions for everyone else in society often do not represent a variety of experiences and perspectives. We need all voices at the table, especially people of the global majority. Bringing diverse perspectives, ideas, scholars of the global majority, and others with various experiences can ensure that outside-of-the box ideas considerations are presented that could lead to new solutions. Third, if you are unaware, you can't be part of the solution. Many of the greatest inequities and challenges in society can benefit from the small changes we each can make daily, as Mr. Robuson shows his scholars. For example, collective effort is almost always needed to improve poverty.

Don't shy away from deep societal issues that might require specialized knowledge. Bring in an expert, bring in community members impacted by the deep societal issues, bring in people who may not have the specialized knowledge, and explore and learn along with your scholars! ●

What Is ISP 4: Recognize and Use Structures in Real-World Systems

Scholars should look for and use structures that occur within STEM so they can use these structures when they encounter new situations to design more efficient solutions to challenges within real-world systems when they encounter new situations. There are four components of this fourth integrated STEM practice:

1. investigate systems across content areas,
2. recognize systems have multiple parts that work together,
3. use models to represent systems, and
4. evaluate the reasonableness of the proposed solution or idea within the context of the system.

By identifying common patterns and structures within STEM systems, scholars can develop a deeper understanding of how these systems work and how different components are connected. This understanding also allows them to apply these structures to new situations and design solutions tailored to the specific task or problem at hand.

Many times in education, when we present "real-world" scenarios, they are overly simplified and not necessarily applicable to scholars' contexts or lives. Furthermore, the scenarios or challenges are often not culturally responsive, especially as it relates to drawing upon scholars' backgrounds, experiences, and interests. For ISP 4, it is first important to understand and define a real-world system. A real-world system is often complex and should be addressed using multiple content areas. A real-world system is often characterized as a messy, wicked problem in which a straightforward solution is not apparent and multiple trials and solutions are necessary. For example, a textbook may ask scholars to construct a fence using 48 yards of perimeter fencing. The "real-world" task is presented as a challenge in which scholars have to maximize the area in which they are fencing. Further, it appears to teachers that it elicits multiple solutions, because there are multiple ways a scholar can create a 48-yard perimeter. However, when we step back and look at the bigger picture, it is a simple system with confined solutions that are not necessarily meaningful to scholars and aren't really adding to their knowledge as societal change agents. Furthermore, if we consider the reasonableness of the solution, is it really reasonable to have a space on a farm that is fenced in by only 48 yards of fencing?

If we were to situate the challenge within a real-world system, scholars would be presented with many more variables and given a real context. Consider the same example above, but from a lens of a horse farm. If scholars are not familiar with horse farms, share video clips and/or photos that will provide scholars knowledge of horse farms. In this context, what if scholars were provided information that a 10-acre farm is looking to fence in a portion of the land to create a paddock area for horses? It might also be helpful for scholars to be given points of comparison so they can envision the size of a 10-acre farm. The farm has a budget of $10,000 to create the fence. The scholars are then provided with a Google map of the farm area where they investigate the best place to put the fence, considering the land structures and landscape. They investigate the types of fences best for horses and begin to build a materials list and construct a model. The model may be a virtual model at first, as they look to maximize the new paddock for the horses. Perhaps the easiest solution is to place the paddock nearest the barn, but that land is full of trees, which would require additional fencing or tree clearing. Differentiation could occur when some scholars investigate the idea that rotational grazing is a key component to future sustainability of our land. Other scholars might investigate how many horses could go within a certain-size paddock and may end up recommending more than one paddock. In all scenarios, scholars are investigating the reasonableness of their solutions, receiving and giving feedback to each other through peer-to-peer interactions, and maybe even presenting their ideas or solutions to area farmers or other community stakeholders to get their feedback on the ideas or solutions, especially as it relates to reasonableness of a solution.

In some learning experiences, scholars may need to be given a different entry point into the real-world system beyond a photo or video clip. In these cases, we encourage educators to consider empathy as an entry point (Edelen et al., 2020). For example, horses or other livestock need a minimum amount of space to grow, play, and have their basic needs met (e.g., eating). The ultimate goal of the fencing is to keep the horses safe, and so providing an entry point through the safety of the horses might help scholars better connect to the real-life context as opposed to just generally thinking about "horse farms." Giving scholars an entry point to a real-world system in which to investigate and provide ideas and solutions helps pave the way for them to collaborate, use multiple content areas, research, build models, and test solutions, all the while building their passion and knowledge. Furthermore, it gives them a real-world basis in which they can truly evaluate the reasonableness of their solution.

It is essential to look at structures within and across content areas when investigating real-world systems. When looking at *systems across the content areas*, it's important to de-center the siloing content areas. This can be challenging in a K–12 school setting because the testing industry and accountability systems found in most of our states drive how our content is structured within the walls of a classroom. Furthermore, students are often presented with the belief there is one right way and that right way is the *only* right way. Whether that's a path to a solution or a definition in a particular context, scholars should be encouraged to find multiple ways to approach an idea or solution. Challenging scholars to draw on their own expertise or others' expertise across multiple content areas, including those outside of the STEM fields, is critically necessary to disrupt the system of belief in one right way, especially when recognizing and using structures to investigate and provide solutions for real-world systems.

It is important for scholars to *recognize that systems have multiple parts that all work together.* See Figure 5.2.

Real-world systems are messy, and while they have many moving parts, all the pieces and parts are necessary to keep the system functioning. The challenge in the multiple parts is finding ways to keep the system functioning efficiently, effectively, and sustainably while making progress toward positive change. Working with scholars to understand the different variables within a particular system will help them to identify how different solutions or ideas impact or not impact an overall system. We must caution ourselves and scholars to avoid getting caught up in thinking more is better than quality, especially when working within iterative cycles. Multiple cycles or trials will be necessary, but it is better to have those trials be well defined. While real-world systems are complex and contain many variables, it is essential to help scholars focus on a cohesive set of variables that allows the challenge to be doable. This looks different across different kinds of systems, but the goals of the system should be shared and discussed. And a preliminary analysis on how the system is currently functioning should be shared with scholars, such as how Mr. Robuson connected insulation systems of animals with the t-chart.

Figure 5.2

Scholars Review Individual Parts of Their Robots to Ensure the Entire Robot Functions as Intended During a Robotics Competition

Source: Julie Sicks-Panus

As scholars look at the structures that make up the system, it's important to consider *models that represent the system* to investigate potential solutions or ideas around improving the system. For our purposes, models can be of three types: visual models (i.e., flowcharts, pictures, diagrams, physical replicas), mathematical models or representations (i.e., symbols representing quantities or equations showing mathematical relationships), and computer models (i.e., simulations). Models can be virtual, physical, or even in some cases two-dimensional. A model gives scholars a tangible draft point from which they can test and refine further ideas and solutions. The focus on models should be to get a draft of an idea or solution and iteratively test it, using the solutions to continue to improve the model. Models are a critical piece of the iterative process we often find in STEM, and more important, we find this in real-world contexts and systems. However, it's vital to have a defined end point when working with scholars in an educational setting to avoid getting caught in a perfectionism cycle. In most cases, we use the term *finished* within a STEM learning experience. However, in a real-life context and situation, *finish* implies that the problem is solved, done, or over with. When working with actual systems, they are never finished. As an educator, you may consider a different word than *finish* to define your end point. It could be "conclusion of model creation," "end of the three trials of cycles," "your most viable solution," and so on. Within STEM learning experiences, we recognize the time constraints we're often under. Further, we want to help scholars continue to make progress and move in a positive direction. In these cases, getting to the end point (e.g., finished) is better than perfect. The end point(s) will likely look different to various groups of collaborative scholars. Having scholars help define what success (or the end point) looks like for the real-world system can help disrupt the cycle of perfectionism.

Finally, it is essential scholars build the capacity to evaluate the reasonableness of their proposed solutions or ideas and build that capacity within the context of the system. Scholars are very creative, and their creativity should be encouraged. Many will present several solutions or ideas in which to approach a challenge or task in a real-world system. Solutions or ideas can be narrowed down by looking at the reasonableness. It's important to consider context when looking at reasonableness. Sometimes a system is constrained by budget, so while the best solution may be more expensive, the reasonable solution will stay within the budget and solve the problem for a long enough time to build the budget to reapproach with the best solution. Considering the reasonableness of solutions holistically enables scholars and their educators to disrupt the system of binary thinking—that is, either/or thinking. It's important to be mindful that evaluating the reasonableness of a solution or idea is not necessarily a linear process in which the evaluation happens at the end, but rather incorporated into the iterative process of recognizing, making use of, and providing solutions and ideas around structures in real-world systems.

Stop, Think, Reflect (5A)

1. How would you describe ISP 4 to a colleague?

2. How would you describe ISP 4 to a scholar engaging in the practice?

 Available for download at **qrs.ly/s9f1lux**

Why Does ISP 4 Matter?

Imagine living in a world where everyday life is simple. What would that look like? Is it even possible for such a world to exist? We know the answer to this question is unequivocally no because complex structures govern the world in which we live. Consider real-world structures or systems you engage in or see on a daily basis. Throughout life, we encounter situations or life events that need to be regulated and solutions sought to effectively and successfully thrive in today's increasingly complex world.

Imagine you are a scientist and that you live in an area where wildfires are a constant threat. You begin thinking about what can be done to mitigate the wildfires and their impact. You sketch a design of an elongated tube connected to a riverbed or ocean because you know that water extinguishes the fire and your design would suppress the spread of the fire. You prepare for an upcoming videoconference call with other STEM professionals who are also thinking about mitigating the effects of wildfires. As the day approaches, you excitedly wait to jump on the call so you can share the news of your design. You begin the call sharing about the spread of wildfires and how it has dramatically increased over the past few months. Leaning into the camera, you loudly whisper that you have a design that would not only extinguish the fires but also mitigate the spread. One of the individuals on the call pipes up and says that they wish they could design something that would curb the derechos, which are hurricane-like storms they have been experiencing in their area. Never before had they had a derecho. In fact, the caller laughingly states, "Who in the world has heard of or even knows what a derecho is?! I haven't. But, I tell you what, we are experiencing times like we have never experienced before." Another caller interjects that they are going through a massive drought. They had gone for months without a single trace of rainfall or any other type of precipitation.

As your colleagues continue to share what is happening in their respective locations, your thoughts go back to the wildfires that are occurring in your area. You begin to wonder, what is the underlying cause of the wildfires? You know your design would help remedy the spread of wildfires, but would it alleviate them? In the middle of your thoughts, a caller reminds the group that you shared a potential solution to mitigate wildfires. They redirect their conversation and express overwhelming support that they should move forward with the design. While the group is excited about your design and the potential of mitigating the wildfires, they also say that the problem is deeper than just wildfires. They are experiencing derechos, droughts, floods, and other devastating weather patterns. "No matter where we live, we are all experiencing an uptick in wildfires, floods, tornadoes, hurricanes, droughts, and sometimes weather events we've never even heard of before," one of the callers says.

Someone then suggests the group take a step back and look at what is happening across the weather system and not solely focus on the weather from their singular vantage point. It is important for everyone to look at the situation holistically so they can determine what solutions would be effective. Another person vouches for the idea and suggests they look at the situation through a scientific lens. Another individual interrupts and says that lens would not be sufficient. Instead, they need to analyze the situation mathematically. Another person interjects and says that that is not sufficient either. They need to consider the people the storms are impacting and how to support the community both mentally and economically. After discussion, they all agree that they cannot rely solely on one content area to design efficient solutions for the climate change everyone is experiencing. The group continues to meet over several months and identifies patterns and relationships among the storms and creates models to represent the systems to test their solutions. They continue to work to design viable, efficient solutions to mitigate the effects of climate change.

While our scholars may not design solutions today on a level to mitigate climate change globally, they need to be able to look for and use structures within a real-world system to design efficient solutions. Such experiences help them see the vast scope and complexity of engaging in this type of thinking—it prepares them for their lives both today and in the future. It is important that scholars have opportunities to apply ideas within and across content areas, examine patterns, use models, and assess the reasonableness of their solution within the given system. When our scholars engage in this practice, they embody empathy as they work toward and collaborate together to design potential solutions that affect an entire system consisting of living and nonliving organisms. Through their active and repeated reasoning, scholars are empowered to seek and develop solutions that would not only bring about change to the immediate challenge but also amplify the productive change within the broader system.

We know that within our society, we are seeking solutions for large-scale and complex problems such as waste management, food insecurity in the community, and preparedness for extreme weather events, to name a few. While we recognize and understand the vastness of these issues, scholars can play a role in addressing these issues within their school communities. For example, scholars might start a recycling program in their school to address concerns about waste management, scholars might establish a food pantry or school garden to provide access to food during the school day, or scholars might develop first aid kits or informational public service announcements to better prepare families for weather events. We argue that engaging scholars in ISP 4 is a stepping stone that allows scholars to be change agents in the world in which they live through analyzing systems holistically to effectively and efficiently design solutions.

●●● SO YOU'VE BEEN TOLD. . . .

Issues in our world need to be solved quickly, faster is better, and resolving a need swiftly is essential.

REALITY CHECK!

In North American culture, the expectation of near-instant solutions is everywhere. We have knowledge and information at our fingertips—so a quick resolution is often seen as essential and advantageous. But sometimes there is a sense of urgency when there doesn't need to be.

Sure, some of life's challenges require immediate action, such as putting out a house fire, moving a turtle from the middle of the road, or avoiding a car accident in a split second. However, many of the longstanding and deeply rooted problems in society are multifaceted, transdisciplinary, and massive in scope and can't be solved quickly. In the story of Mr. Robuson and his unit on biomimicry, scholars quickly realize one person, one action, or one change will not completely eliminate the issue, but they are positioned as solution-seeking change agents toward improvement. In fact, Mr. Robuson's scholars realize the issue can never fully be solved but that they can get involved by providing solutions through the annual coat and glove drive.

Realizing some inequities or aspects of life can't be fully solved is a hard but important lesson for scholars. Just as important is the idea that there are still valuable ways to contribute to solutions and advocate for such causes. Scholars need a safe space to dive into some of society's most pressing issues and explore and learn about them. ●

- How did you see Mr. Robuson engage scholars in ISP 4? What specific actions did he use throughout the task?
- How did scholars use models in the task?
- How were scholars encouraged to make designs more efficient?
- What systems across content areas were evident in the task?

 Available for download at **qrs.ly/s9f1lux**

Diving Deeper: Mr. Robuson as a STEM System Disruptor

In the biomimicry task, scholars began an inquiry with a field trip to the local zoo to learn about how animals are insulated for warmth. Mr. Robuson challenges the STEM status quo ideas of either/or and progress is bigger/more. As the scholars saw at the zoo, there is not a simple answer for how animals are insulated for warmth. In their designs, Mr. Robuson encouraged them to continue being open to multiple options so that they did not oversimplify the task. Mr. Robuson also challenged the idea of progress is bigger/more by focusing on efficiency. Thus, scholars not only had to think about how to create an effective insulation system, but they also had to think about how to do so using the fewest materials.

Mr. Robuson leveraged the background knowledge from the zoo to connect to the annual coat and glove drive to build **empathy**.

Centering the inquiry in the scholars' locality evoked caring about the local community in which they lived. Whether it is the scholars' own community or one they learn about from afar, building empathy engages learners to want to understand and seek solutions to improve their surroundings. Mr. Robuson connected the learning to the annual coat drive to evoke emotion and a sense of wanting to help the situation, which engaged scholars as part of the solution.

With that empathy building, Mr. Robuson recognized the need to focus on solution seeking for those in need. Mr. Robuson quickly turned the focus of the lesson to designing effective insulation systems and communicating what worked best. Mr. Robuson wanted scholars to come away with a sense of individual and collective action to **empower** them

to know their thoughts and actions can make a positive difference.

Each scholar may not be able to donate a coat to the coat drive, but as a group, they could share what they learned about insulation to encourage others to donate the warmest coats for those in need. Moreover, the scholars were empowered as a collective group when Mr. Robuson helped them set a goal for the coat drive and think about why the goal was reasonable. This mathematical reasoning helped scholars develop their mathematical reasoning and justification abilities.

There was a natural need to know about how systems work when designing an insulation system. By encouraging scholars to see individual parts and how the parts work together, Mr. Robuson was developing scholars' **dispositions** to use systems thinking when analyzing problems.

Scholars also collaborated, used critical thinking, and engaged in making and doing, all of which are critical dispositions for scholars to develop when actively participating in STEM learning experiences.

●●● SO YOU'VE BEEN TOLD. . . .

There is always a correct or best solution.

REALITY CHECK!

This is such a deeply ingrained part of a traditional school experience, for us as scholars and as educators. While prevalent in all STEM disciplines, it is especially dominant in mathematics learning. Sure, simple and noncontextual problems can have exactly one correct solution (e.g., the solution to an equation, the slope of a line, the perimeter of a figure), but the beauty of mathematics and STEM is in the contextual application to society's biggest, messiest challenges, which often do not have a correct or best solution. Life is often much more complicated. In fact, a single scenario often reveals many practical, social, financial, and emotional variables that lead to complex consideration of options and possible paths forward.

Helping your scholars embrace the complexities of ISP STEM tasks is a great gift to them. Nurturing flexibility in thinking where scholars recognize there might be multiple perspectives and solutions, as well as learning that sometimes when others choose a different path, there isn't always a right or wrong way, will greatly contribute to the intellectual and emotional growth of your scholars. ●

Putting ISP 4 Into Action: What Does It Look Like?

Scholars look for and use structures in real-world systems and assess the reasonableness of their solution within the context of the system. In Table 5.1, we describe what engagement in ISP 4 would look like in the classroom.

Table 5.1

Putting ISP 4 Into Action

	COMPONENTS TO ISP 4	TEACHER ACTIONS	SCHOLAR ACTIONS
ISP 4: Recognize and use structures in real-world systems	Investigating systems across content areas	Engage scholars in tasks that require the use of multiple disciplines. Make explicit connections to cross-cutting concepts in solution seeking.	Identify where scholars apply science, technology, engineering, and/or mathematics concepts. Look for and use patterns that arise when using the design process.
	Recognizing systems have multiple parts that work together	Facilitate guided explorations of systems, to include an emphasis on subsystems. Provide opportunities for scholars to explore efficiency in design.	Explain how parts of a system work together to make the system work. Look for patterns and ways to simplify designs while meeting the goal.
	Using models to represent systems	Introduce scholars to effective models. Engage scholars in critiqueing and identifying limitations of models.	Create and use models as a way to communicate ideas. Compare models to real world. Identify limitations of models.
	Evaluating the reasonableness of the proposed solution or idea within the context of the system	Identify stakeholders and explore their perspectives. Guide scholars to evaluate multiple solutions in real-world systems.	Evaluate multiple ideas or solutions. Consider stakeholders and the potential impact on them.

Assessing ISP 4

Mr. Robuson assessed scholars through the guided exploration and discussion from the zoo field trip. To communicate a clear purpose, Mr. Robuson asked scholars to look for specific characteristics of animals that would help them survive in different environments. Scholars took their design notebooks so they could sketch their observations and record them for later use. The following day, Mr. Robuson asked scholars to share what they observed. This informal assessment allowed Mr. Robuson to gauge scholars' understanding of how specific animal characteristics help animals survive in their habitats. Through that discussion, Mr. Robuson used a scholar's question to launch the design challenge.

Throughout the task, Mr. Robuson observed and questioned scholars working to design an insulation system. He observed scholars collecting data on whiteboards and refining their designs. He asked how scholars were inspired by nature to reinforce the idea of biomimicry. He also assessed scholars by having groups share recommendations for insulation systems, which he recorded at the end of the design lesson. Mr. Robuson then helped scholars communicate their recommendations for insulation systems as they made posters for the school's coat and glove drive. This process helped Mr. Robuson assess what scholars learned about their designed insulation systems, as scholars' recommendations focused on important parts within the system.

●●● SO YOU'VE BEEN TOLD . . .

Solutions need to result in a new product, something additional, or something more than what is currently being done.

REALITY CHECK!

We live in a more is more society. But sometimes less is really more, and sometimes a solution is right in front of us, even though we might not see it. Engaging your scholars in the ISPs in ways that focus on removing harmful factors (for example, creating more waste rather than repurposing), cutting back, reducing waste, simplifying, and focusing on quality over quantity will help scholars embrace this important lesson in life. For example, less processed food, a less busy schedule, food as preventative medicine rather than taking more and more medication in some cases, less stuff in our homes, less stress, and vehicles, plastics, and production that are less harmful to the environment. Sometimes the solutions we seek can be found in "less" rather than something more or new. ●

In the Moment Feedback

In the Moment Feedback is a tool that educators can use as they assess scholars on ISP 4. The first set of questions are formative assessment questions meant to generate a discussion among and between you and your scholars. Such discussions will help you gain an understanding of where scholars are and what additional supports they might need as they engage in ISP 4. The Design Notebook Prompts are prompts you can provide your scholars for them to respond in writing to facilitate literacy and written communication, encourage engineering design thinking processes, and serve as a record of activity similar to what is often expected in the workforce. We encourage the use of the design notebook that showcases scholars' growth on ISP 4.

Formative Assessment Questions (teachers asking scholars)

Purpose: In the Moment Feedback

- What are the key components to the system you are analyzing?

- How are the components connected to one another? If I take this component out or change it, what happens to the system?

- What feedback loop can you build into the system? If you could pick out one piece of the system to give you data or feedback on, what would it be? Why did you pick that piece?

Design Notebook Prompts (scholars complete individually or in groups)

Purpose: Continuous record of learning experiences/final showcase of work

- Draw a map or picture that identifies the key components of the system and how they are connected.

- Draw a picture or describe what happens when you take out (remove) one component of the system. Would it look the same or different? If different, does it look like another system you know?

- Draw a picture or represent with a model one pattern you noticed within the system.

- If you could change one thing about the system, what would it be and why?

- Who or what does the system positively impact?

- Who or what does the system negatively impact? How would you address the negative impact?

 Available for download at **qrs.ly/s9f1lux**

ISP 4 RUBRIC

In Table 5.2, we provide a rubric that you can use to assess your scholars' engagement in ISP 4.

Table 5.2

ISP 4 Rubric

ISP 4 COMPONENTS	NEEDS MORE SUPPORT	APPROACHES EXPECTATION	MEETS EXPECTATION	ACHIEVING SOCIETAL CHANGE AGENT
Investigating systems across content areas	There is not yet evidence that multiple content areas were investigated within the system.	Two or more content areas were used in the solution or idea, but it is not yet clearly defined as to the contribution of the areas.	Three or more content areas were used to investigate the real-world system in order to generate solutions or ideas. Research of potential ideas or solutions is evident.	Three or more content areas were used to investigate the real-world system and the content areas are clearly evident in the ideas or solutions (e.g., integrated content areas).
Recognizing systems have multiple parts that work together	There is not yet evidence that the multiple parts or structures of a system have been considered.	Multiple parts to a system are evident, but it is not yet clear how the variables or parts work together within the system.	Describes and articulates how multiple parts of a system, including the different variables, work together. Ideas or solutions based on the behavior of the variables are presented clearly.	Describes and articulates multiple parts of a system with justifications of how the parts work together. Variables are clearly defined and organized in a way that helps the reader make sense of the system through a big picture lens.
Using models to represent systems	A model is not presented, considered, or not yet clear. It does not address or capture the different variables or structure of the system.	A model is presented, but it only addresses a limited number of variables within the system.	A model is presented and addresses a reasonable number of variables so as to present a solution or idea.	A model is presented and addresses a reasonable number of variables within the storied context of a solution or idea for the real-world system challenge.

(Continued)

(Continued)

ISP 4 COMPONENTS	NEEDS MORE SUPPORT	APPROACHES EXPECTATION	MEETS EXPECTATION	ACHIEVING SOCIETAL CHANGE AGENT
Using models to represent systems (continued)		The model is not clear in presenting an idea or solution. The model may not have the ability to iteratively test and improve an idea or solution within the real-world system.	The model has the ability to iteratively test and use the results to improve the solution or idea within the real-world system. The model is well organized and clearly communicates the idea or solution.	The model has the ability to iteratively test and use the results to improve the solution or idea within the real-world system. The model is well organized and presents the solution or idea within a storied context that takes into account the big picture real-world system.
Evaluating the reasonableness of the proposed solution or idea within the context of the system	The reasonableness of a solution or idea is not yet considered within the context of the real-world system.	Multiple ideas or solutions are considered for their reasonableness, but justifications are not yet included for how or why they were chosen or not chosen or they were the best fit or not the best fit.	Multiple ideas or solutions are considered for their reasonableness and the justifications are included. The justifications address different scenarios present in the real-world system.	Multiple ideas or solutions are considered for their reasonableness and the justifications are included. The justifications address different scenarios present in the real-world system and allow the stakeholder to consider how to best maximize their structures within the real-world system. The reasonableness of a solution or idea considers the context of the real-world system, including the stakeholders and the potential impact on them.

Stop, Think, Reflect (5C)

1. How could you use ISP 4 in your own classroom?

2. How could you turn a current lesson into one that engages scholars with ISP 4?

 Available for download at **qrs.ly/s9f1lux**

 **Recap This!**

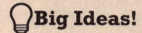 **Big Ideas!**

ISP 4

Recognize and use structures in real-world systems

Engaging scholars in real-world place-based learning evokes caring, which helps to foster scholars' **empathy**.	When scholars are positioned to make a positive difference and learn about the advocacy of citizen scientists, scholars feel **empowered** to be part of the solution.
Scholars become **agents of change** when they examine the entire system and not just individual components. By examining the entire system, scholars see there are multiple solutions to a challenge and there is not just one way to solve it.	Encouraging scholars to think creatively and outside of the box when solving challenges cultivates positive **dispositions** and **empowers** scholars to become **agents of change**.

●●● STEM STARTERS

- Jump into societal issues that can never fully be solved! In the story of Mr. Robuson, scholars learned that they could not fully fix or eliminate poverty; they could help others by making recommendations to donors during their annual coat drive, using what they learned about biomimicry. Scholars need to come to accept the truth that some of life's biggest challenges will always exist, yet important and impactful changes can be made to make progress toward short- and long-term change. In short, scholars will take away that they can be instrumental in making a difference!

- You can deeply engage in the ISPs and disciplines of STEM even if you aren't the "expert" or have all the answers! The biggest STEM challenges we face are complex and specialized. It is understandable to feel you don't know enough about the topic to engage in learning about it with your scholars. We encourage you instead to shift your thinking toward access. Even if it's not perfect, even if you are learning along with your scholars, even if you don't have all the answers, even if you need to enlist help, engage your scholars anyway!

- Celebrate multiple perspectives! Strategically ensure scholars see multiple possible impactful solutions and ideas. Celebrate diversity in thinking and focus. This builds flexibility and classroom community and respect for ideas different from the scholars' own ideas. ●

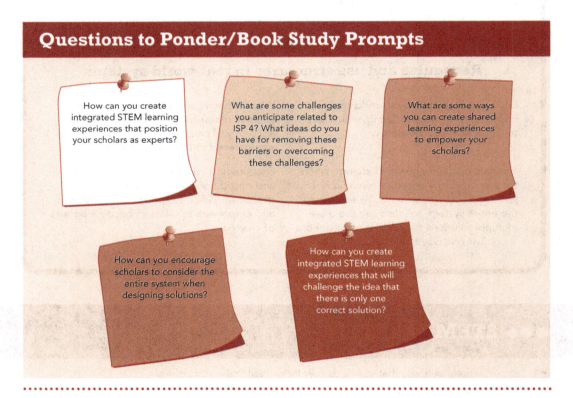

Questions to Ponder/Book Study Prompts

How can you create integrated STEM learning experiences that position your scholars as experts?

What are some challenges you anticipate related to ISP 4? What ideas do you have for removing these barriers or overcoming these challenges?

What are some ways you can create shared learning experiences to empower your scholars?

How can you encourage scholars to consider the entire system when designing solutions?

How can you create integrated STEM learning experiences that will challenge the idea that there is only one correct solution?

online resources ↘ Available for download at **qrs.ly/s9f1lux**

TRY THIS!

Whether you're trying a new STEM task or reimagining one you've used in the past, try the following in Table 5.3 to highlight the aspects of ISP 4 we have discussed in this chapter.

Table 5.3

ISP 4: Recognize and Use Structures in Real-World Systems

COMPONENTS TO ISP 4	ASPECTS OF TASK	QUESTION PROMPTS FOR SCHOLARS
Investigating systems across content areas	Investigations come from multiple disciplines or require the use of multiple disciplines in order to provide solutions.	What ideas from science, technology, engineering, and mathematics can you use to design a solution?
	Highlight cross-cutting concepts embedded in solution seeking.	What patterns did you notice when you tested your idea? What do the patterns tell you?
Recognizing systems have multiple parts that work together	Provide opportunities to identify repeated reasoning, including relationships between and among topics.	How do you know if your system is successful? What are things you can change in your system? What variables (things that you can change) are present in the system? How does changing one part impact how other things work? Does the change impact one part or multiple parts? Is there a relationship between or among the variables? What variables might have the most impact on the system? What variables might be missing from the system?
	Explore systems to improve efficiency, define success within various contexts, and improve sustainability.	What could be eliminated or reduced in order to make your system better? How can you make your system last a long time (sustainability)? Improve efficiency or sustainability? Is the system effective in different contexts (e.g., places, situations)?
Using models to represent systems	Use models to represent real-world systems.	How can you create a model to describe the system? (Note—Encourage physical, virtual, or two-dimensional models.) Are the parts labeled? How do the parts work together? (Note—Encourage creativity in models—work to disrupt the idea of perfectionism in designing the model.)
	Iteratively test the model (e.g., compare and contrast models, peer feedback, stakeholder feedback, iterative revisions).	What are the constraints of the model? How does the model provide for iteratively testing a solution or idea?
		How can the model be improved based on previous tests or feedback from stakeholders?
		How efficient is the model? Can efficiency be considered and achieve the same success criteria for the real-world system?

(Continued)

(Continued)

COMPONENTS TO ISP 4	ASPECTS OF TASK	QUESTION PROMPTS FOR SCHOLARS
Evaluating the reasonableness of the proposed solution or idea within the context of the system	Consider the reasonableness of an idea or solution.	Is the solution or idea reasonable? Is the solution or idea cost-effective? Efficient? Sustainable?
	Consider the reasonableness of an idea or solution with stakeholders.	Is the solution or idea a short-term or long-term solution? Does the solution consider factors holistically (e.g., societal, ethical, cultural)? Does the solution or idea impact stakeholders differently in various contexts? What context maximizes the solution or idea? What context minimizes the solution or idea? What context eliminates the solution or idea? What context, while implementing the solution or idea, creates a new real-world system problem that will need a new solution or idea (e.g., domino solution or idea)?

REIMAGINING EXISTING STEM TASKS

Throughout this book, you have gotten to know, discuss, and practice the four ISPs that help to answer the question teachers and STEM education professionals most often have: What does *doing* STEM in my classroom or setting actually look like?

What Does It Mean to *Do* STEM?

Facilitating rich, integrated STEM experiences inside or outside of the classroom can sometimes feel like a daunting task. Sometimes you may not feel qualified to facilitate in this way, maybe because you didn't have similar transformative experiences yourself as a scholar, or maybe you weren't prepared to teach in this way in your own teacher preparation program. Oftentimes, as teachers, we want to be perfect and facilitate instructional tasks that we feel comfortable and "qualified" to teach. But this way of thinking only perpetuates the notion of perfectionism. Instead, we, as STEM system disruptors, must challenge the STEM status quo idea of perfectionism and the idea that only "qualified" persons can lead or facilitate rich, integrated STEM tasks. Our goal throughout our previous work and within this book has been to disrupt the STEM status quo by providing explicit and tangible examples and descriptions of what *doing* STEM looks like in everyday classrooms and other educational settings. And let's be real, we can't ask our scholars to be uncomfortable and embrace the "not knowing" if we aren't willing to do the same!

The four Integrated STEM Practices (ISPs), with which you are now very familiar, are critical components of high-quality STEM learning experiences. When successfully implemented, these ISPs allow scholars to apply discipline-specific content and practices, including across multiple disciplines, to authentic learning experiences, especially those that reside within real-world systems. In turn, when scholars have access to these high-quality integrated STEM learning experiences, they begin to develop or continue to cultivate positive STEM identities and productive dispositions. While we want all scholars to love engaging in STEM, it is not our goal to have every scholar pursue a STEM career (although it's wonderful when they do decide to take that path). Rather, our goal is for every scholar to have an appreciation for STEM, a deeper understanding of STEM concepts, and feel empowered to use STEM in meaningful ways in their lives. We envision scholars being able to use the practical skills within the ISPs to apply ideas from within and across contexts, especially drawing upon their own integrated STEM content experiences. Further, approaching integrated STEM learning in this way allows scholars to apply discipline-specific content through rigor, discourse, and purpose. Participating in these high-quality STEM learning experiences empowers scholars to be positioned as competent, contributing members of their communities, within or outside of STEM, and to use their knowledge, skills, and dispositions to be societal change agents. This, in turn, can continue to empower scholars to pioneer innovative and inclusive ways of learning and working together.

What Are High-Quality STEM Tasks and Learning Experiences?

A high-quality STEM learning experience or task engages scholars as the agents who are *doing* the work by engaging collaboratively in creative and critical thinking to provide solutions or ideas for real-world system challenges by *actively using multiple content areas* where stakeholder voice, culture, and impact are positively centered. When considering the transformation or implementation of a task or experience, consider Figure 6.1.

STEM Beyond the Walls of the Classroom

When creating, reimagining, or implementing STEM tasks, we as teachers often take on much of the burden of that work. It's our nature as educators. We're expertly prepared in the creation and implementation of curricular resources and materials, so why would that be any different when implementing STEM tasks or experiences? When thinking about creating high-quality learning experiences, we usually have three core questions we center upon:

- What do I want to do with my scholars—and *why*?
- Why are my scholars doing this task?
- What do I want my scholars to know and be able to do—and *why*?

Figure 6.1

Designing Learning Experiences Using the Equity-Oriented STEM Literacy Framework Components

Critical Thinking & Problem Solving
- Are the scholars doing the work?
- Are scholars collaboratively seeking solutions situated in real-world contexts?
- How are multiple ISPs present in the work the scholars are doing?
- How are scholars drawing from multiple content areas during the task or experience?

Utility & Application
- Are scholars able to connect the results of their work to other facets of their personal experiences? To other real-world systems?
- Are intentional uses of existing materials being considered?

Empathy
- Are scholars connected to the purpose of the work? In other words, does the real-world challenge or system *mean* something to them?
- How are scholars considering stakeholders? Are they considering who is being included? Are they considering who is being left out?
- Does the experience include time and pathways for scholars to consider how those most impacted by the challenge feel? How does the solution(s) bring about positive or negative change to their lives?
- How does the learning experience or task scenario engage scholars in "feeling with" another.

Dispositions
- At the end of a task or experience, is curiosity sparked? Are scholars left wanting to investigate more?
- Are scholars positioned in such a way that they are positioned to take initiative on the experience or task?

STEM Identity Development
- How are you helping scholars overcome perfectionism in this task or experience?
- How are scholars positioned as qualified experts within the task?
- How are scholars' sense of belonging in STEM developed through the experience? Are scholars seeing themselves as a STEM expert "in the moment" of the task or challenge?

Empowerment
- How are scholars given opportunities to provide thoughtful feedback that enables others to improve their ideas and walk away feeling empowered?
- How are scholars empowered to investigate and explore different possible solutions or ideas?

As with all instructional task development, it's critical to make sure there is a clear purpose and alignment to the work we're asking our scholars to do. It might be tempting for educators just to search the Internet for "STEM elementary lessons"—in which case a whole list of various hands-on activities appear. But these lessons often lack purpose, structure, and coherence—especially related to the intended learning outcomes, progressions, or standards for the grade level or program. It's important to ensure the experiences we're presenting to scholars are high quality. Otherwise, we're not truly cultivating opportunity and access.

When centering on the three questions, we can ensure purpose in terms of alignment to core ideas related to the course or program and an alignment to learning outcomes, progressions, and standards. In our prior work, Bush et al. (2020) studied scholars' perceptions of their STEAM learning experiences and found there is a hierarchy of integrated STEAM learning experiences. The least impactful were primarily disconnected, non-empathy-driven hands-on activities, with little or no clear connection to STEAM content and practices. The most impactful learning experiences were authentic, transformative empathy-driven learning experiences that both ignited a passion in scholars and necessitated meaningful application of STEAM content and practices. By engaging deeply in the ISPs grounded in our Equity-Oriented STEM Literacy Framework, we can move away from disconnected "fun activities" to transformative empathy-driven STEM learning experiences and capture the real meaning of STEM in the hearts and minds of our scholars.

When it comes to creating high-quality ISP learning experiences, we encourage educators to actually practice the four ISPs themselves in the creation of the tasks. Still further, we advocate for another educator-focused ISP: Leveraging the Community (ISP +1).

What Is ISP +1: Leveraging the Community?

In Leveraging the Community, educators take into consideration all the different possible resources and connections that could help bring additional connections to the task or challenge, especially related to the Equity-Oriented STEM Literacy Framework. When thinking about leveraging the community, this could truly encompass anything and anyone—colleagues, families, community members, industry partners, business partners, government officials, town or city officials, neighbors, and so on. The hardest part of leveraging the community? Asking!

Asking for help is the biggest challenge because we educators are vulnerable to fulfill a desire or need for our scholars. To overcome this potential roadblock, ask yourself: What's the worst thing that can happen with an ask? The answer: The worst thing that can happen with an ask is that the person(s) says no. Also consider the fact that you won't get to a yes without asking. Although a no answer can sting or feel defeating, at least it's a definitive answer, and you can move on and potentially pursue other ideas. Without asking in the first place, you are stalled from the start.

Here are some tips to consider when leveraging the community:

- Tip 1: Start out a written request with a very short paragraph outlining the purpose of your task or challenge and the intended outcome. Hint: This paragraph should succinctly answer the questions of what you want to do with your scholars and why your scholars are doing this task or challenge.

- Tip 2: Make a list of required resources you're requesting. Try a two-column approach: One column will list the *must haves* and the other column will list items that will *extend the task or challenge.*

- Tip 3: Maximize your chances of success by thinking of ways to leverage the community that do not require money (either donations or purchasing of supplies). Industry or business partners often have volunteer time and would love to come give peer feedback or answer questions, serving as experts in the field. Indeed, community partners may have a particular challenge: they would like scholars to seek solutions. And you might be well served to ask partners what they are interested in doing. After all, partnerships should be mutually beneficial!

- Tip 4: Use your favorite search engine to look for specific terms or outcomes related to your task or challenge and see who or what in your area is doing similar work. Then reach out!

- Tip 5: Don't forget to circle back! Whether it's through a thank you card from your class or a showcase of learning to show off the scholars' work, always reach back out to showcase the end results and help forge future connections or partnerships.

Taken together (Figure 6.2), Leveraging the Community (ISP +1) and the four ISPs, you can truly transform instructional work in STEM into high-quality, creative, and inquisitive learning environments that collectively challenge every scholar.

Figure 6.2

Relationship between ISPs and Equity-Oriented STEM Literacy Framework in Creating Rich, Equitable STEM Tasks

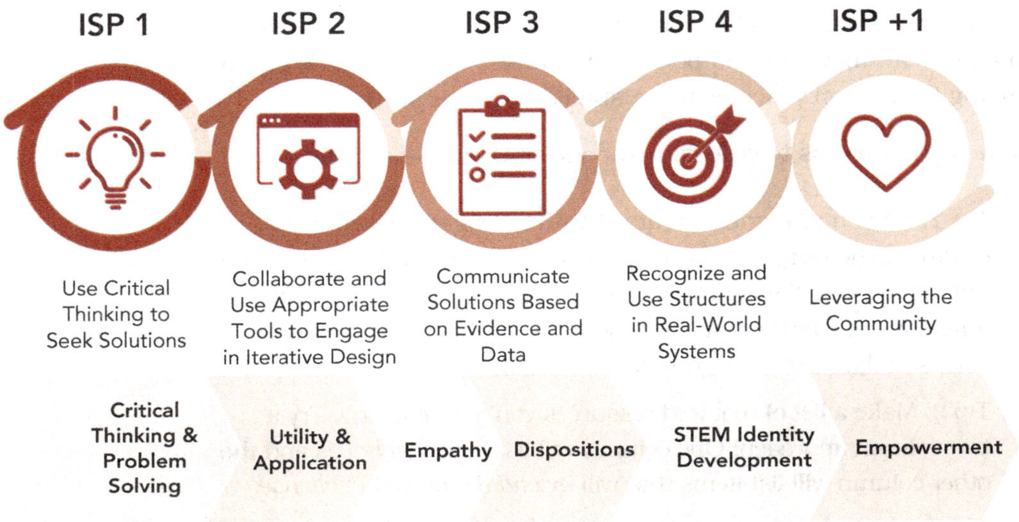

ISP 1	ISP 2	ISP 3	ISP 4	ISP +1
Use Critical Thinking to Seek Solutions	Collaborate and Use Appropriate Tools to Engage in Iterative Design	Communicate Solutions Based on Evidence and Data	Recognize and Use Structures in Real-World Systems	Leveraging the Community
Critical Thinking & Problem Solving	Utility & Application	Empathy Dispositions	STEM Identity Development	Empowerment

Source: light bulb and target icon by istock.com/Avector; browser icon by Istock.com/Ersa Sen Kula; checklist icon by Istock.com/Elvinagraph.

STEM Challenge

Now that we have set the stage for creating or transforming a STEM learning experience, let's dive a little deeper into what this can look like with an example challenge. Consider the famous marshmallow tower STEM challenge that we've seen floating around on social media websites or we may have seen or done as teachers and scholars ourselves. In this STEM challenge, scholars are usually given toothpicks and marshmallows and asked to build the tallest structure possible. Other variations include using spaghetti, and sometimes variables are constrained such as limiting the number of materials and supplies. On the surface, it appears this STEM task encourages scholars to use critical and creative thinking, collaborate with other scholars, and communicate their ideas and solutions. However, it's missing the key component of what are the scholars doing and *why?* In other words, as typically implemented, it's one of those disconnected "fun activities" we mentioned earlier. The *why* should encompass empathy, applicability, and utility in STEM, defining and solving actual challenges in our world, as well as looking at real-world systems.

So how can we transform this task—we admit that it's a lot of fun to build something out of toothpicks and marshmallows!—into a high-quality transformative empathy-driven STEM learning experience?

WHAT DO I WANT TO DO WITH MY SCHOLARS AND WHY?

In undertaking this task, do you want to focus on particular content or concepts? Do you want to take a disconnected "fun activity" and translate that to a meaningful, empathy-driven STEM learning experience? Do you want to build a short experience or investigation around a particular issue or idea? Whatever your rationale, articulate the reasoning and build from there. In this case, let's say we want our scholars to experience collaborating together and using STEM intentionally to build a structure out of toothpicks and marshmallows.

WHY ARE MY SCHOLARS DOING THIS?

Finding scholar motivation for STEM learning is often where teachers and educators can get stuck. We read or hear about what sounds like a great task and we want our scholars to experience it, but there may not be an obvious or direct connection to why our scholars should undertake it. In these cases, we might go back to the content that our scholars are learning or that we're tasked with teaching in our classrooms and thus begin a deep circular dive into the content abyss where we start to question the connection of any of our tasks or ideas.

RECOGNIZE AND USE STRUCTURES IN REAL-WORLD SYSTEMS (ISP 4)

Instead, think about the connection to real-world systems first, as a beginning point. Let's think about towers in the real world: Quickly jot down two to three ideas that come to mind when you think about towers in the real world. You might have come up with something like this:

- Leaning Tower of Pisa
- Skyscraper
- Cellphone tower
- Radio tower
- Wind turbine
- Light pole
- Electrical pole

The list can go on and on. Looking at *your* list of real-world towers, what jumps out at you as something that would interest your scholars most? Maybe a cellphone tower? If you are unsure what would be most interesting, don't be afraid to poll or ask your scholars! You can use the same approach with them: When you think of towers, what do you think of? This is a great way to capture the interests of your scholars and build connections with them to help bridge their interests with the content in your setting. See Figure 6.3.

Figure 6.3

Scholars Share the Tallest Tower They Could Make From Three Pieces of Paper

So let's focus on the cellphone tower. While we've defined the cellphone tower as a possible real-world system, we still haven't defined the *what* or *how* of the task. This is where thinking about the course content can be useful. Perhaps you are studying waves in your science classroom. You might want to use the task of building a marshmallow tower to emulate building a cellphone tower and then use the model as a vehicle to study different types of waves and their purpose, lengths, and so on. Perhaps in mathematics, you're studying three-dimensional solids and so you want to use the cellphone towers as an example of a prism. Perhaps in environmental science, you are studying carbon footprint and want to study the extraordinarily high carbon footprint the cellphone tower has due to its traditional use of diesel-powered generators. Making these content connections helps us to connect to the purpose behind the task.

USE CRITICAL AND CREATIVE THINKING TO SEEK SOLUTIONS (ISP 1)

At the planning stage, you have the opportunity to differentiate instruction based on personalization and scholar choice. Most often in educational settings, we're taught that to differentiate instruction, we have to take a particular task and create different versions of it, usually shortening or extending the task or work. When we focus on the scholar as the driver and initiator, we're able to listen to the scholar define how they best view the task and personalize it to their experiences. It's easy to think we are giving the scholars a pass and that they'll always choose the easiest path (they don't always!). However, we as educators can still build on additional challenges within the initial ideas the scholars present.

In our cellphone tower case, let's explore waves. If you want to do a focused STEM task, be specific in talking about the kinds of waves cellphone towers emit. Are they the same or different from other towers, such as radio towers? What other kinds of waves exist and for what purpose? Then you can talk about wavelengths, how far they travel, and what happens to the waves as they travel. You could do some simple sound wave tasks in the classroom or slinky representations or models.

But what task are we trying to solve? Perhaps the challenge we're trying to solve is how far apart to put the cellphone towers. But there are different variables. Perhaps one group is looking at cellphone towers in the Great Plains area. Another group is looking at cellphone towers within the Appalachian Mountains. Another group is looking at cellphone towers in the Pacific Northwest. The challenge could be related to cellphone access in these areas and the need to build additional towers to increase reliable service in the various geographical areas.

COLLABORATE AND USE APPROPRIATE TOOLS TO ENGAGE IN ITERATIVE DESIGN (ISP 2)

When planning your task, think about the different ISPs you want your scholars to engage in. As you've probably noticed in reading through this resource, the ISPs can build upon each other and play with each other across a variety of tasks and experiences. While you don't have to implement all of the ISPs every time with a particular task, it's good practice to focus on and incorporate multiple ISPs together in a task or experience. Shorter tasks might focus on one to two ISPs, and longer tasks or experiences might encompass three to four ISPs: There are no hard-and-fast rules around this.

So going back to our cellphone task, we've already identified we want our scholars to use toothpicks and marshmallows to build a cellphone tower. Further, we should think about the different variables our scholars will be facing in their planning and solution seeking. In the mountains, they'll have to consider terrain and snowfall. In the Great Plains, they'll have to consider the wind and droughts. In the Pacific Northwest, they'll have to consider rainfall and terrain. What kinds of tools will scholars need to investigate and collaborate together? Do they need access to the library media center? Do they need access to a search engine, or are there specific resources you want to point them to use? Do you have paper, crayons, markers, rulers, and so on to help draw up a plan? Do you have maps of the area?

COMMUNICATE SOLUTIONS BASED ON EVIDENCE (ISP 3)

When planning a STEM task or experience, it's essential to think about how the solutions or ideas will be communicated. Leaving it up to scholar choice is both easy and appropriate because scholars often have great ideas on how to communicate their ideas or solutions. It's our job as educators to help guide them to create their solutions or ideas based on evidence and data, focusing objectively on the real-world system, no matter how they are communicated. See Figure 6.4.

Within the context of our cellphone tower example, the marshmallow and toothpick structures can be one piece of the communication

Figure 6.4

Scholars Present Their Design and Receive Feedback From Their Peers

Source: Tracy Young

of the solution or idea. Scholars will probably want to build multiple, smaller towers on a posterboard or particular area in the educational setting to represent the different spacing ideas for the towers. The structures may vary from place to place, as one of the variables we identified earlier was landscape and weather conditions. With the toothpick towers as their models, scholars can make claims using evidence and reasoning about their designs. They can identify how their models simulate the real-world system but also identify limitations of their models.

As scholars begin to communicate their solutions or ideas, it's important to incorporate peer feedback into the process. While the scholars have been collaborating together as a team, it's essential to model the outside feedback mechanism ever present in real-world systems. Providing structure and modeling respect with the feedback is critical to ensuring we are not weaponizing feedback in our classroom setting. Encourage scholars to use the following language when providing feedback:

1. "I wonder . . ." (when they have an idea or addition or change)

2. "I like . . ." (when they want to encourage a group to keep an idea)

3. "I have a question . . ." (when they would like to know more about a particular solution or idea)

Structuring feedback in this way, or similarly, models respectful collaboration and feedback, and it empowers scholars to share their ideas and thoughtfully consider others' ideas.

In turn, it is important to help scholars understand how to receive feedback. Encourage the receiving scholars to use the following when receiving feedback:

1. Acknowledge the feedback. "Thank you for sharing. . . ." "Thank you for sharing your idea. . . ." "We had not yet considered that. . . ."

2. Have scholars sort through the feedback. Feedback could be given via sticky notes, index cards, poster paper, and so on. Encourage scholars to determine how feedback can be sorted into useful information toward improving the idea, solution, model, and so forth.

3. When incorporating the feedback, acknowledge where you incorporated the feedback.

Finally, not all feedback is good feedback, and that's okay. It's important to not focus on the quality of the feedback in determining if it is useful or not. If a feedback suggestion will not work, it is okay to put it aside and move on to the next.

LEVERAGING THE COMMUNITY (ISP +1)

Threaded throughout the planning of a task should be consideration of what resources are available. This key component is about leveraging the community within your task or experience. The community is defined broadly: your school staff community, your school parent and family community, the community in which you live, and so on. When thinking of leveraging the community, teachers or educators often shy away because they feel like it's asking for help or perhaps they will be seen as unqualified. This is untrue! When we reach out to our communities, we are inviting them into our conversations and ideas about education and what's happening in our classroom and educational settings. Especially in thinking about the community at large, our communities often want to get involved but don't know how or are not sure where to start with an offer to help.

In thinking about our cellphone tower task, we might reach out to our local cellphone provider to see if they have an engineer or tower expert on hand to come talk with the scholars or share resources they have. Or you might reach out to your local government planning official because cellphone towers usually have partnership and land agreements for usage. They have to go through local government processes for planning, approval, and inspections. Local planning officials can also speak to the distance, size, weather conditions, and other variables scholars might have considered in their planning. You could also reach out to an environmental expert who might share some of the environmental impacts cellphone towers have in their areas. Don't worry if you don't know any names or have no contacts. As we discussed before, you can always put the key ideas into your favorite search engine and start there! Further, share your ideas with your colleagues and oftentimes, if they know someone, they will eagerly share that information with you!

Community partners have knowledge about how resources are being used and by whom. Oftentimes, this can help educators identify access and equity challenges for people across a community, especially for people of the global majority. For example, our cellphone providers know who is able to access reliable service and who is not. They also are able to share what challenges providers face when trying to expand access to reliable service. When scholars understand the accessibility aspects to equitable services for all, from both the community/consumer and the provider/industry aspect, this helps to build empathy within their task or challenge. For example, when scholars realize how not having access could have true social, financial, and/or health implications for an individual, they are more likely to feel empathetic and more likely to understand equitable access.

As we know from the Equity-Oriented STEM Literacy Framework, empathy is an essential component in building STEM learning experiences. Centering on empathy helps to ensure the collaboration, partnership, or ask is mutually beneficial. If you are struggling in this area, brainstorm with your scholars. Our scholars oftentimes are able to offer perspectives from both sides that we as adults might not consider.

Keep the Ideas Flowing

In this chapter, we have focused on reimagining STEM tasks. We have looked at considerations for high-quality STEM tasks and specifically focused on how they embody the ISPs. Within the cellphone tower example above, we showcased how scholars might develop their abilities across multiple ISPs simultaneously while also using the ISPs (+1) as a framework for transforming or creating a STEM task or experience.

CONSIDER THIS!

Throughout the text, we presented each ISP in depth at its own chapter (see Figure 6.5 for a recap). As you read through the various stories and examples, you probably started to see the connections among the ISPs. This is by design: ISPs are not meant to be viewed in isolation but rather to be used together intentionally throughout the tasks or learning experience. Although the ISPs do intentionally build upon each other, there is no rank or order to the ISPs. They can operate independently of one another or be incorporated together. So how do you know which ISP to focus on? Let your outcomes drive which ISPs you choose. Take into consideration:

- *The scope of the STEM learning experience.* Smaller or shorter tasks or challenges may benefit from a focus on one to two ISPs. Larger or longer tasks may lend themselves easier to all four ISPs.

- *The outcomes for your scholars.* While a content outcome may be the desire, what ISPs will help to propel the content forward in meaningful ways within the task?

- *The needs and desires of your scholars.* Using your formative data, including personal connection with scholars, you can decide which ISPs to focus upon for particular tasks or experiences.

Next up are a roadmap and conversation starters that will further assist you (or you and your team) through the planning, implementation, and assessment of a high-quality STEM learning experience.

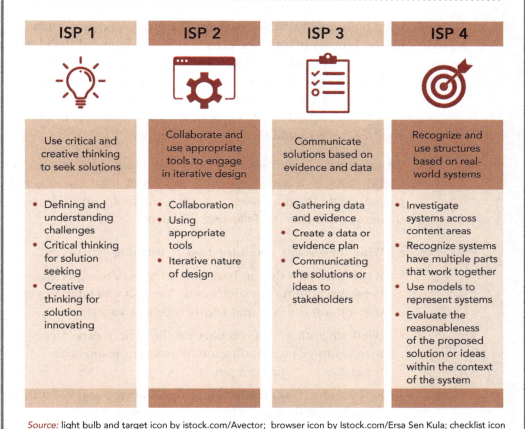

Figure 6.5

ISPs and Their Components

ISP 1	ISP 2	ISP 3	ISP 4
Use critical and creative thinking to seek solutions	Collaborate and use appropriate tools to engage in iterative design	Communicate solutions based on evidence and data	Recognize and use structures based on real-world systems
• Defining and understanding challenges • Critical thinking for solution seeking • Creative thinking for solution innovating	• Collaboration • Using appropriate tools • Iterative nature of design	• Gathering data and evidence • Create a data or evidence plan • Communicating the solutions or ideas to stakeholders	• Investigate systems across content areas • Recognize systems have multiple parts that work together • Use models to represent systems • Evaluate the reasonableness of the proposed solution or ideas within the context of the system

Source: light bulb and target icon by istock.com/Avector; browser icon by Istock.com/Ersa Sen Kula; checklist icon by Istock.com/Elvinagraph.

You'll have the opportunity to complete the STEM planning tool, try out some of the resources, and plan for how you will assess scholars' learning. Most important, we continue to ground this work in the components of the Equity-Oriented STEM Literacy Framework.

ISP PLANNING DOCUMENT

Use the following planning guide to help create or transform your STEM task or experience that incorporates the ISPs. We encourage using this guide for STEM learning experiences of all different scopes—small or large! Adapt the guide as needed to help best fit your context. We highly encourage using multiple ISPs in addition to intentionally incorporating multiple content areas, even if it feels uncomfortable for you as an educator. The purpose of the guide is to ensure key components of ISPs are present and to spur additional creativity and planning for your STEM tasks or experiences. This planning document is not meant to be a new lesson or unit plan format, but rather, guiding questions to help plan what your high-quality STEM task or learning experience might look like and things to consider. After you have completed the planning document, you should incorporate it into your favorite lesson or unit plan format. We have included a copy of all the example ISP rubrics (see Table 6.2), from each chapter, together after the planning tool (see Table 6.1). We hope this will be useful in planning your assessment and design pieces together.

We encourage you to openly share your ideas, brainstorms, and STEM tasks or learning experiences with at least one other colleague. Invite them to listen to a short pitch of your idea and ask them to respond to the following questions:

- What do you like about the task or learning experience?

- What questions do you have about the task or experience— these are refining questions only. They should be trying to understand the how and why of a task or experience.

- What suggestions do you have for the task or experience— we encourage peer feedback to phrase suggestions as "I wonder . . ." For example,

  - I wonder if you might call the local library and see if they will come do a short tutorial on a makerspace?

  - I wonder if Mr. Gonzales would have some posterboard you could use?

  - I wonder if you had the scholars go outside and take pictures, and then they could cut out what they find.

This feedback session can take place multiple times if needed. It can be as short as 10 minutes or as long as 30 minutes. It also doesn't have to be in formal spaces, although it is important that the space is created in such a way that voices and presence are honored. See Tables 6.1 and 6.2.

Table 6.1

ISP Planning Tool

Integrated STEM Practices	Centering Equity-Oriented STEM Literacy Framework	Disrupting the STEM Status Quo
• 1—Use critical and creative thinking to seek solutions • 2—Collaborate and use appropriate tools to engage in iterative design • 3—Communicate solutions based on evidence and data • 4—Recognize and use structures in real-world systems	• Dispositions—curiosity, initiative, persistence, etc. • STEM identity development—positioning in tasks and as experts • Empowerment—scholar voice, space for initiative, encouragement • Critical thinking and problem solving • Utility and application—usefulness, connection to real-world systems • Empathy—stakeholder voice, positive or negative impact of stakeholders, who is being left out, who is benefiting	• Avoid binary thinking • Focus on quality, not quantity • Intentional collaborative groups where all voices have space and are heard (avoid power hoarding) • Scholars doing the work and tasks • Scholars using critical thinking and creative thinking as much as possible • Embrace and empower multiple solutions and ideas instead of one right way • Focus on finished success criteria and less on perfect success criteria—careful attention to avoid perfectionism • Define progress as quality iterations instead of more iterations or more ideas • Focus on empowering voice and ideas and less on what qualifications are necessary

Here's a form you can use or adapt to help in brainstorming:

Brainstorm initial ideas
What is it that you want the scholars to *do*?
What task or challenge do you want your scholars to seek solutions to? Is it a common or unique question or challenge? Is it a challenge unique to a particular scholar or group of scholars or particular community, and so on?

(Continued)

(Continued)

How does this task or challenge connect with scholars? Will scholars be interested in seeking solutions to this task or challenge? If not, can you tweak your brainstorm to something they would be interested in or relate to? Is there cultural relevance to the solution they are seeking? Is there a personal or community connection?

Refine the initial idea here

What are the materials needed for the STEM learning experience or task?

Are there community or school resources you wished you had for this task or experience?

What kinds of constraints or guardrails do you need to put on the task or experience across all groups/persons?

How will scholars communicate their design processes? Will they have a design notebook? Are they expected to write out ideas, solutions, reflections, and/or draw pictures? Will they be allowed to take pictures or video? How will you accommodate the various communication preferences of scholars?

How do you want to give feedback to scholars? Will you collect and write in their design notebooks? Will you give sticky note feedback? Will you give video comments or audio comments as feedback?

What rubric(s) will you use? What modifications do you need to make to accommodate your task or experience? (See end of this section for example rubric.)

What does defining the challenge look like for your task or experience? What are you looking for? Where might your scholars encounter roadblocks or struggle?

What does it look like for your scholars to analyze, evaluate, and synthesize information (aka, critical thinking) for this task or experience? Be sure to think about each of these pieces individually as well as holistically.

What does it look like for your scholars to investigate, imagine, and innovate (aka, creative thinking) for this task or experience? Be sure to think about each of these pieces individually as well as holistically.

How will scholars know they have succeeded with the task or experience?

How will you know your scholars have succeeded?

How do you expect your scholars to share the results of their task or experience?

Are there any additional accommodations you might need to consider along the way?

 Available for download at **qrs.ly/s9f1lux**

Table 6.2

Comprehensive Integrated STEM Practices Rubric

KEY AREA OR COMPONENT	NEEDS MORE SUPPORT	APPROACHES EXPECTATION	MEETS EXPECTATION	ACHIEVING SOCIETAL CHANGE AGENT
Identifying the challenge (Critical thinking)	Challenge and context are not yet mentioned. It is unclear what is being investigated.	Challenge is vaguely defined. Context may or may not be present. While a broken or nonfunctioning object is present, it is vague regarding the challenge.	Challenge is specifically defined for the project. The criteria for how the object is supposed to work are clearly defined. Constraints are somewhat considered.	Challenge is specifically defined as well as the constraints. Goals for the object are specific and able to be tested.
Identifying solutions (Creative thinking)	Only one solution is constructed for the challenge.	Describes a few solutions but it's not yet clear how they will be carried out.	Describes multiple solutions with a plan for how to carry them out. For example, ranking how the solutions should be approached.	Describes multiple solutions with justifications. Understands the constraints of the solutions and has a plan for carrying them out.
Testing and revising solutions (Critical and Creative thinking)	Solution is not yet tested or there is no plan for testing.	Tests and makes changes to solutions, but there is not yet a clear path to the ultimate solution. The different trials do not yet build on each other or prior results.	Uses an iterative process to test different solutions. Carefully documents and plans each test based on the results of the previous test.	Uses an iterative process to test different solutions, taking into consideration each previous test and additional constraints learned along the way. The process is carefully documented.
Common understanding of task (Collaboration)	There is no common understanding of the goal of the task.	While able to describe the task, is unable to describe the goal of the task.	Describes the goal of the task.	Describes the goal of the task and assists peers in ensuring they have the same understanding of the goal.

KEY AREA OR COMPONENT	NEEDS MORE SUPPORT	APPROACHES EXPECTATION	MEETS EXPECTATION	ACHIEVING SOCIETAL CHANGE AGENT
Conflict management strategies (Collaboration)	Does not use appropriate conflict management strategies.	Attempts to use conflict management strategies but gets defensive and/or does not listen to peer feedback.	Uses conflict management strategies without getting defensive. Writes down peer feedback in design notebook.	Uses conflict management strategies without getting defensive. Uses peer feedback to improve solution or idea.
Use of appropriate tools	Does not use available tools or is not able to explain why a tool is appropriate to use.	Chooses appropriate tools to use but is not able to fully explain why the tools are appropriate for the task.	Chooses appropriate tools to use and fully explains why the tools are appropriate for the task.	Chooses the appropriate tools to use and fully explains why the tools aid in efficiency and effectiveness for the task. Suggests additional tools that might have been even more helpful to use or try.
Iterative design	Does not engage in multiple trials of the solution. Provides ideas or solutions but does not test them.	Provides ideas or solutions and completes one test. Does not use the results to improve the solution.	Provides ideas or solutions and completes at least two tests. Uses the results to improve the solution before testing another time.	Provides ideas or solutions and completes multiple iterations of testing until the goal is achieved for the task. Results are used to improve the solution each time.
Design notebook	Has a design notebook but does not use it for recording ideas, feedback, test results, and final results.	Has a design notebook and records some of the ideas, feedback, and test results. Missing pieces to the iterative process.	Has a design notebook that has a running record of ideas, solutions, feedback, test results, change ideas, and final results.	Has a design notebook that has a running record of ideas, solutions, feedback, test results, change ideas, and final results. There are sketches, clear connection of change ideas to test results, and ideas for future solutions based on the final result.

(Continued)

(Continued)

KEY AREA OR COMPONENT	NEEDS MORE SUPPORT	APPROACHES EXPECTATION	MEETS EXPECTATION	ACHIEVING SOCIETAL CHANGE AGENT
Gathering data or evidence	Data or evidence are not collected or only one type of data is collected. It is unclear how the data or evidence were collected.	Multiple data or evidence are collected. It is somewhat unclear how the data or evidence were collected. Data and evidence are disorganized. Some stakeholder voices were left out.	Describes and articulates how multiple data or evidence are collected. Data or evidence are organized in such a way to be able to look at and draw conclusions. Stakeholders' voices are included throughout.	Describes and articulates multiple data or evidence collected with justifications. Data and evidence are organized to look at and draw conclusions. Whose voice might be left out of the stakeholders was considered and then captured in the data and evidence.
Creating a data or evidence plan	Data or evidence being collected are not clear. No research has been completed that might have pointed to solutions or ideas. It is unclear what the goal or what success looks like for the solution or idea.	Data or evidence plan are vaguely defined. Some research has been conducted. It is unclear if the stakeholders were considered in the plan.	Data or evidence plan are clearly defined. Variables have been considered. Research of potential ideas or solutions is evident. Stakeholders are considered in the plan.	Data or evidence plan are specifically defined as well as the constraints or variables. Multiple data or evidence are considered. All stakeholders are included in the plan with a rationale.

KEY AREA OR COMPONENT	NEEDS MORE SUPPORT	APPROACHES EXPECTATION	MEETS EXPECTATION	ACHIEVING SOCIETAL CHANGE AGENT
Communicating* the solutions or ideas to stakeholders **Communication can mean oral, written, mixed media, video, or another form of communication that serves to tell the story.*	Communication of the solution or idea does not yet include data or evidence.	Communication is organized and present but does not yet objectively showcase data or evidence used for creating solutions or ideas. The impact on the stakeholders is unclear.	Communication is organized and presents multiple representations to the different possible solutions or ideas, what tests or trials or models were completed, the results, and reflection. Impact on stakeholders is present throughout.	Communication is organized and presents a clear story of the idea or solution. Solutions and ideas are objectively presented and feedback is listened to and rebutted (if necessary). It elevates the voices of all stakeholders, including the impact on them. It offers recommendations for future iterations of the solutions or ideas and possible models that might predict outcomes.
Investigating systems across content areas	There is not yet evidence that multiple content areas were investigated within the system.	Two or more content areas were used in the solution or idea, but it is not yet clearly defined as to the contribution of the areas.	Three or more content areas were used to investigate the real-world system in order to generate solutions or ideas. Research of potential ideas or solutions is evident.	Three or more content areas were used to investigate the real-world system and the content areas are clearly evident in the ideas or solutions (e.g., integrated content areas).
Recognizing systems have multiple parts that work together	There is not yet evidence that the multiple parts or structures of a system have been considered.	Multiple parts to a system are evident, but it is not yet clear how the variables or parts work together within the system.	Describes and articulates how multiple parts of a system, including the different variables, work together. Ideas or solutions based on the behavior of the variables are presented clearly.	Describes and articulates multiple parts of a system, with justifications of how the parts work together. Variables are clearly defined and organized in a way that helps the reader make sense of the system through a big-picture lens.

(Continued)

(Continued)

KEY AREA OR COMPONENT	NEEDS MORE SUPPORT	APPROACHES EXPECTATION	MEETS EXPECTATION	ACHIEVING SOCIETAL CHANGE AGENT
Using models to represent systems	A model is not presented, considered, or not yet clear. It does not address or capture the different variables or structure of the system.	A model is presented, but so far it only addresses a limited number of variables within the system. The model is not clear in presenting an idea or solution. The model may not have the ability to iteratively test and improve an idea or solution within the real-world system.	A model is presented and addresses a reasonable number of variables so as to present a solution or idea. The model has the ability to iteratively test and use the results to improve the solution or idea within the real-world system. The model is well organized and clearly communicates the idea or solution.	A model is presented and addresses a reasonable number of variables within the storied context of a solution or idea for the real-world system challenge. The model has the ability to iteratively test and use the results to improve the solution or idea within the real-world system. The model is well organized and presents the solution or idea within a storied context that takes into account the big picture real-world system.
Evaluating the reasonableness of the proposed solution or idea within the context of the system	The reasonableness of a solution or idea is not yet considered within the context of the real-world system.	Multiple ideas or solutions are considered for their reasonableness, but justifications are not yet included for how or why they were chosen or not chosen or they were the best fit or not the best fit.	Multiple ideas or solutions are considered for their reasonableness and the justifications are included. The justifications address different scenarios present in the real-world system.	Multiple ideas or solutions are considered for their reasonableness and the justifications are included. The justifications address different scenarios present in the real-world system and allow the stakeholder to consider how to best maximize their structures within the real-world system. The reasonableness of a solution or idea considers the context of the real-world system, including the stakeholders and the potential impact on them.

 Available for download at **qrs.ly/s9f1lux**

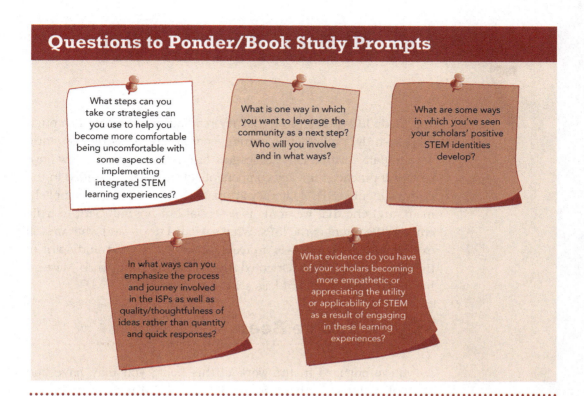

What steps can you take or strategies can you use to help you become more comfortable being uncomfortable with some aspects of implementing integrated STEM learning experiences?

What is one way in which you want to leverage the community as a next step? Who will you involve and in what ways?

What are some ways in which you've seen your scholars' positive STEM identities develop?

In what ways can you emphasize the process and journey involved in the ISPs as well as quality/thoughtfulness of ideas rather than quantity and quick responses?

What evidence do you have of your scholars becoming more empathetic or appreciating the utility or applicability of STEM as a result of engaging in these learning experiences?

online resources

Available for download at **qrs.ly/s9f1lux**

CHAPTER 7

THE HEART AND SPIRIT

You made it! Whether your journey reading this book was through a book study, professional learning community, a district- or state-wide initiative with a close colleague, or on your own, you now have read and practiced the key components of the ISPs, grounded in the Equity-Oriented STEM Literacy Framework. This is a big accomplishment, and one that we argue is essential but not sufficient to truly embody the intent of the ISPs. What's needed next—and what we will explore in this chapter—is an exploration of the heart and spirit of the ISPs and the Equity-Oriented STEM Literacy Framework. More on heart and spirit soon, but let's set the stage first.

Where You've Been

As you've engaged in the work of this book, you may have had to think differently about your role as a STEM teacher or leader. You've likely brainstormed how to remove barriers from our traditional education norms—many of which have been deeply rooted in classrooms. For example, this might include uprooting the notion of competitiveness to find the "best" solution. This notion is problematic because:

1. There might be multiple strong solutions that should be considered for different reasons or situations. Life is often much more complicated than the notion of one "best" or "right" solution due to the many practical, social, financial, and emotional variables that coexist in our world.

2. The belief that perfectionism is essential to make meaningful contributions is simply not true. Striving for excellence is different from perfectionism.

The best solutions in society are often a compilation of so many perspectives and contributions, all needed, but often very "drafty" and messy along the way. In these moments, you are acting as a STEM System Disruptor!

Along your journey to discovering more about the ISPs and the Equity-Oriented STEM Literacy Framework, you've likely had to

146

reconsider the role of the STEM educator—shifting from the "knower" to one who provides scholars the opportunities and pathways to explore and learn in divergent and creative ways. You may have found your scholars have also been uncomfortable with shifts in their roles. This makes sense as they likely have long been required to act, contribute, and perform in very narrow ways to be successful in a traditional school environment. Perhaps scholars didn't even embrace their elevated voices and more equalized status (as in Wood et al., 2019) at first; maybe they continued to lean on you as the teacher for every step to take and for specific "answers." Through this process, you may have needed to reassure and push them to develop different ways of thinking as they engaged in the ISPs.

We want to reassure you that any feelings of being uncomfortable treading in these unchartered waters—waters that are messy and beautiful and thrive on creativity and individuality and community—is a sign of progress. This process won't be swift and clean. But with the messiness comes the potential for extraordinary impact. Feeling the discomfort of Equity-Oriented ISPs is good and a necessary part of the growth.

This process won't be swift and clean. But with the messiness comes the potential for extraordinary impact.

Shifting Away From a Checklist Mindset Toward an ISP Mindset

In Chapter 1, we introduced you to the Equity-Oriented STEM Literacy Framework and the four ISPs. Chapters 2 to 5 unpacked each ISP and provided classroom stories of their implementation, connected deeply to practice standards, busted myths, and posed important questions. Chapter 6 took a closer look across the ISPs and introduced ISP +1, providing a roadmap for implementation. You are fully equipped with all the tools you need to make this shift! However, there is still one aspect that is deeply ingrained in our being as educators that needs to be released: the infamous checklist approach to teaching. We've all been in the habit of checking things off our to-do list, but we recommend taking a breath and resetting toward a mindful and reflective approach. We invite you to take a moment to pause your reading and go grab a sheet of paper and a pen or pencil. On the paper, write the words "to-do," "checklist," and "quantity." When you finish, make sure the paper is lying flat and grab the top part of the paper and start crumpling it into a circular wad. Now, you are ready for the grand finale! Grab a wastebasket (aka trash can), and make a dramatic slam dunk. Feel free to create your own trademark slam dunk or extend Vince Carter's, Michael Jordan's, or Dwight Howard's. Exhale. Take a much-needed sigh of relief. You got this!

Now you are fully equipped to shed the checklist mentality and move toward a reinvigorating, transformed ISP mindset. Let's take a moment to reflect on the ISP learning experiences you've read about, tested out, and implemented with your scholars since beginning this journey.

Stop, Think, Reflect (7A)

1. How did implementing an ISP make you feel as an educator?
2. What was the energy in the classroom?
3. How did scholars describe their experiences?
4. What did scholars take away from the ISP learning experiences?
5. How did your teaching shift?
6. How did scholars' learning shift?

 Available for download at **qrs.ly/s9f1lux**

This newfound approach is not something to do in addition to or separate from regular instruction. Instead, it's an embodiment of how we engage scholars in the STEM disciplines and practices. It is a way of being. It is who we are.

Now, grab a sticky note in your favorite color. Write the words "ISPs," "heart," and "spirit" on the sticky note. Place the sticky note in a place where you'll be constantly reminded of the main ideas presented in this book.

Heart and Spirit

The two key ingredients of the ISPs and Equity-Oriented STEM Literacy Framework are the embodiment of the heart and spirit of this work.

The *heart* of this work includes a deeply rooted belief

- In the brilliance all scholars bring to the classroom community
- In a sense of flexibility, openness, and nurturing approach to working with scholars
- That when we leverage scholars' strengths and lived experiences, everyone in the classroom community learns and benefits (including us!)

The *spirit* of this work includes a classroom community that derives its energy from

- Collective knowledge, progress, and success
- A caring and nurturing learning approach where scholars feel safe and are excited to take risks, be iterative in their thinking, and messiness is celebrated
- Strengths that are leveraged as vehicles for change and advocacy

From our perspective, truly embodying this work boils down to

- Positioning scholars as learners, doers, and advocates
- Elevating the voices of scholars
- Equalizing the status of scholars
- Diversifying perspectives and ensuring different ideas are seen as strengths
- Ensuring we interact with scholars in a loving and nurturing way
- Being a warm demander (check out Berry's Corwin Connect blog on this topic, 2021) in our push for scholars' brilliance
- Leveraging scholars' uniqueness as beautiful gifts
- Embracing the art of "unlearning" as so much of what we do in school has been so deeply ingrained in all that we do.

We also want to provide some tangible examples of how often we, as educators (us included!), have implemented practices that are well intentioned but actually perpetuate norms that run counter to the embodiment of this journey. In Table 7.1, we provide Embraceable Equity-Oriented Alternatives for you to consider as you embark on the implementation of the ISPs in your teaching.

Table 7.1

Embraceable Equity-Oriented Alternatives

WHAT SEEMS WELL INTENTIONED	HOW IT'S ACTUALLY PROBLEMATIC	EMBRACEABLE EQUITY-ORIENTED ALTERNATIVE
Giving all scholars the exact same access	While well intentioned, scholars bring different strengths and entry points into the conversation and need different supports to be successful.	Leverage scholars' unique strengths to make STEM content, practices, and contexts accessible.
Rewarding flawless or perfect solutions	While believing in the brilliance of your scholars is foundational to this work, rewarding scholars that specifically showcase their brilliance in seemingly flawless or perfect ways is foundationally flawed. It perpetuates competition, overfocuses on the product and underfocuses on the process, and devalues collective contributions.	Allow scholars to showcase the contributions to the process and solution in ways that celebrate each other and collective contributions.
Guiding scholars toward "the right solution"	It may seem you are helping scholars by strategically guiding them toward a solution you believe will be successful, but this practice is problematic for several reasons. First, it perpetuates the idea of one right solution, which just isn't true in life. Second, this strategy removes individuality, creative thinking, and the solution-seeking process from the STEM task.	Keep your ISP STEM learning experience open and exploratory. Sure, you might have to provide a suggestion or pose a question to scholars for them to continue to make progress, but don't strip the beauty and creativity from a learning experience!
Showcasing only a few scholars' work	While giving scholars feedback can be positive, if you only showcase a particular scholar's work or way of thinking, especially too soon, it may strip the creativity and solution-seeking mindset out of other scholars who think the showcased work is the only "correct" way and abandon their own attempts.	Allow scholars to preview and peer review each other's work through collaboration and discourse. This allows scholars to see a variety of ways to tackle a problem and ask each other "I wonder," clarification, and elaboration questions. Be in the habit of showcasing many different approaches.

WHAT SEEMS WELL INTENTIONED	HOW IT'S ACTUALLY PROBLEMATIC	EMBRACEABLE EQUITY-ORIENTED ALTERNATIVE
Grading on the final product and ignoring the process	Oftentimes, we get in a rut of grading final solutions that scholars provide and not diving deep into the process of how they got there. The learning is happening throughout the learning experience or investigation, and all stages should be assessed with constructive feedback and celebrated.	Use a rubric to assess scholars at multiple steps in their inquiry process. You could have multiple "checks" throughout their process to provide them with feedback. Value the process.
Sticking with the same resources, learning experiences, and assessments year after year	Our world is constantly changing and evolving, and so are the scholars that come to our classrooms every day. We must adapt the resources that we use throughout to better meet their needs and make their learning more relevant. We know that teacher burnout is real, and we can often get stuck in our ways. After all, building new learning experiences or resources can take some time, and that is something that we don't have a lot of as teachers. But in reality, not changing with the times is doing our scholars a great disservice and a disservice to future generations as well.	You don't have to re-create the wheel, and you don't have to do it alone! Start with one topic (or go bigger and incorporate a full unit) and think about ways you can adapt what you already have to be more relevant and inclusive for all scholars. Reach out to other teachers in your building, instructional support team(s) at your school or at the district level, or even the community of teachers from your local teacher prep program. Chances are, someone has an idea of how you can extend a learning experience to include all STEM fields and implement the ISPs, even if you are stuck.

Why Us?

Why are we responsible to change the STEM status quo? Why are we the STEM System Disruptors? Why do we bear this burden? Given the vast technological advances; inequities that continue to be perpetuated locally, nationally, and globally; and the challenge of sustainability in a world of limited resources, increased costs and expenses of living, and steep competitiveness, we absolutely must inspire and equip this generation to be their own best advocates. We as educators have the greatest opportunity for the most wide-span, systematic, equitable reach and impact. We can't afford to miss this opportunity.

As a collective, we as educators have the ability to provide opportunities and experiences to every scholar—including the global majority—so that they are equipped to push back on dominant cultural norms that negatively impact all. Through collective efforts, the next generation just might be able to build a future where very different ideas take hold in our culture, where multiple ways of thinking are appreciated, all voices are heard, and quality and care take precedence over quantity. Above all, humans will be valued for who they are as humans.

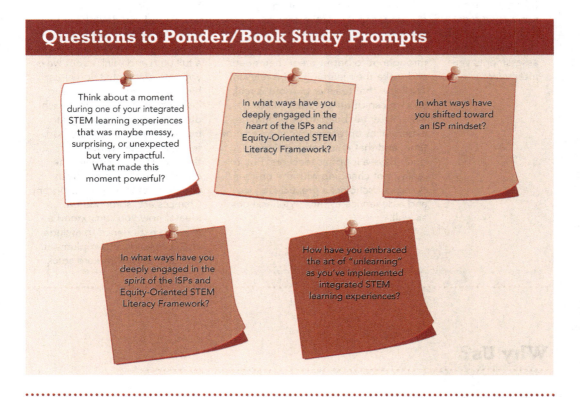

Questions to Ponder/Book Study Prompts

Think about a moment during one of your integrated STEM learning experiences that was maybe messy, surprising, or unexpected but very impactful. What made this moment powerful?

In what ways have you deeply engaged in the *heart* of the ISPs and Equity-Oriented STEM Literacy Framework?

In what ways have you shifted toward an ISP mindset?

In what ways have you deeply engaged in the *spirit* of the ISPs and Equity-Oriented STEM Literacy Framework?

How have you embraced the art of "unlearning" as you've implemented integrated STEM learning experiences?

online resources — Available for download at **qrs.ly/s9f1lux**

REFERENCES

Aish, N., Asare, P., & Miskioğlu, E. E. (2018). *People like me: Providing relatable and realistic role models for underrepresented minorities in STEM to increase their motivation and likelihood of success* [Conference session]. 2018 IEEE Integrated STEM Education Conference (ISEC) (pp. 83–89), Princeton, NJ, USA.

Berry, R. Q., III. (2021). Three ways being a "Warm Demander" is culturally responsive and supports students' mathematical identity and agency. *Corwin Connect Blog Post.* https://corwin-connect.com/2021/03/three-ways-being-a-warm-demander-is-culturally-responsive-and-supports-students-mathematical-identity-and-agency/

Bostic, J. D., Matney, G. T., & Sondergeld, T. A. (2019). A validation process for observation protocols: Using the revised SMPs look-for protocol as a lens on teachers' promotion of the standards. *Investigations in Mathematics Learning, 11*(1), 69–82. https://doi.org/10.1080/19477503.2017.1379894

Brennan, K. (2017). Designing for learning by creating. *International Journal of Child-Computer Interaction, 14,* 7–9. http://doi.org/10.1016/j.ijcci.2017.06.003

Bullock, E. (2017). Only STEM can save us? Examining race, place, and STEM education as property. *Educational Studies, 53*(6), 628–641. https://doi.org.csulb.idm.oclc.org/10.1080/00131946.2017.1369082

Bush, S. B., & Cook, K. L. (2018). K-12 STEM and STEAM education in the United States: Vision and best practices. *Teachers College Record.* Record Number: 22533.

Bush, S. B., & Cook, K. L. (2019). *Step into STEAM: Your standards-based action plan for deepening mathematics and science learning.* National Council of Teachers of Mathematics.

Bush, S. B., Cook, K. L., Edelen, D., & Cox, R. (2020). Elementary students' STEAM perceptions: Extending frames of reference through transformative learning experiences. *The Elementary School Journal, 120*(4), 692–714.

Bush, S. B., Edelen, D., Roberts, T., Maiorca, C., Ivy, J. T., Cook, K. L., Tripp, L. O., Burton, M., Alameh, S., Jackson, C., Mohr-Schroeder, M. J., Schroeder, D. C., McCurdy, R. P., & Cox, R., Jr. (2022). Humanistic STE(A)M instruction through empathy: Leveraging design thinking to improve society. *Pedagogies: An International Journal, 26*(4), 111–129. https://doi.org/10.10 80/1554480X.2022.2147937

Bybee, R. W. (2010a). Advancing STEM education: A 2020 vision. *Technology and Engineering Teacher, 70*(1), 30–35.

Bybee, R. W. (2010b). What is STEM education? *Science, 329*(5995), 996. https://doi.org/10.1126/science.1194998

Bybee, R. W. (2013). *The case for STEM education: Challenges and opportunities.* NSTA Press.

Bybee, R. W. (2018). *STEM education now more than ever.* National Science Teachers Association.

Consortium for Mathematics and Its Applications (COMAP) and Society for Industrial and Applied Mathematics (SIAM). (2019). *GAIMME: Guidelines for assessment and instruction in mathematical modeling education* (S. Garfunkel & M. Montgomery, Eds., 2nd ed.). COMAP and SIAM.

Cook, K., Alameh, S., Tripp, L., Maiorca, C., Schroeder, C., & Mohr-Schroeder, M. (2021). Reimagining the five practices for effective and equitable discourse: An example from a virtual STEM experience. *Connected Science Learning 3*(3).

Cook, K. L., Bush, S. B., & Cox, R. (2017). From STEM to STEAM: Incorporating the arts in roller coaster engineering. *Science and Children, 54*(6), 86–93.

Cook, K. & Bush, S. (2015). Structuring a science-mathematics partnership to support pre-service teacher's data analysis and interpretation skills. *Journal of College Science Teaching, 44*(5), 46–52

Edelen, D., & Bush, S. B. (2021). Moving towards inclusiveness in STEM with culturally responsive teaching. *Kappa Delta Pi Record, 57*(3), 115–119. https://doi.org/10.1080/00228958.2 021.1935178

Edelen, D., Bush, S. B., Simpson, H., Cook, K. L., & Abassian, A. (2020). Moving towards shared realities through empathy in mathematical modeling: An ecological systems theory approach. *School Science and Mathematics, 120*(3), 144–152. https://doi.org/10.1111/ssm.12395

Gay, G. (2018). *Culturally responsive teaching: Theory, research, and practice* (3rd ed.). Teachers College Press.

Graf, N., Fry, R., & Funk, C. (2018, January 9). *7 facts about the STEM workforce.* Pew Research Center. https://www.pewresearch.org/fact-tank/2018/01/09/7-facts-about-the-stem-workforce

Hawthorne, B. (2022). *Raising antiracist children: A practical parenting guide.* S&S/Simon Element.

Henriksen, D. (2014). Full STEAM ahead: Creativity in excellent STEM teaching practices. *The STEAM Journal, 1*(2), 15.

International Technology and Engineering Educators Association (ITEEA). (2020). *Standards for technological and engineering literacy: The role of technology and engineering in STEM education.* https://www.iteea.org/STEL.aspx

Jackson, C., Mohr-Schroeder, M. J., Bush, S. B., Maiorca, C., Roberts, T., Yost, C., & Fowler, A. (2021). Equity-oriented conceptual framework for K-12 STEM literacy. *International Journal of STEM Education, 8*(38), 1–16. https://doi.org/10.1186/s40594-021-00294-z

Kelley, T. R., & Sung, E. (2017). Sketching by design: Teaching sketching to young learners. *International Journal of Technology and Design Education, 27,* 363–386.

Kobett, B., & Karp, K. (2020). *Strengths-based teaching and learning in mathematics: 5 teaching turnarounds for Grades K–6.* National Council of Teachers of Mathematics.

Krutsch, E., & Roderick, V. (2022). *STEM day: Explore growing careers.* U.S.

Department of Labor Blog. https:// blog.dol.gov/2022/11/04/stem-day-explore-growing-careers

Love, T. S., Wells, J. G., & Parkes, K. A. (2017). Examining the teaching of science, and technology and engineering content and practices: An instrument modification study. *Journal of Technology Education, 29*(1), 45–65. https://doi.org/10.21061/jte.v29i1.a.3

Maharaj, S., & Campbell-Stephens, R. (2021, February 9). We are not visible minorities; we are the global majority. *Toronto Star.* https://www.thestar.com/opinion/contributors/2021/02/09/we-are-not-visible-minorities-we-are-the-global-majority.html

Mohr-Schroeder, M., Bush, S. B., Maiorca, C., & Nickels, M. (2020). Moving toward an equity-based approach for STEM literacy. In C. Johnson, M. J. Mohr-Schroeder, T. Moore, & L. English (Eds.), *Handbook of research on STEM education* (pp. 29–38). Routledge.

Moll, L. C., Amanti, C., Neff, D., & Gonzalez, N. (1992). Funds of knowledge for teaching: Using a qualitative approach to connect homes and classrooms. *Theory Into Practice, 31*(2), 132–141.

NASA. (2018). *BEST engineering design model.* https://www.nasa.gov/audience/foreducators/best/edp.html

National Governors Association Center for Best Practices & Council of Chief State School Officers. (2010). *Common core state standards: Mathematics.* National Governors Association and Council of Chief State and School Officers. http://www.corestandards.org/Math/

National Research Council. (2011). *Successful K-12 STEM education: Identifying effective approaches in science, technology, engineering, and mathematics.* National Academies Press.

National Research Council. (2012). *A framework for K-12 science education: Practices, crosscutting concepts, and core ideas.* National Academies Press.

National Science and Technology Council. (2018). *Charting a course for success: America's strategy for STEM education.* A Report by the Committee on STEM Education of the National Science & Technology Council. https://www.whitehouse.gov/wp-content/uploads/2018/12/STEM-Education-Strategic-Plan-2018.pdf

NGSS Lead States. (2013). *Next generation science standards: For states, by states.* The National Academies Press. www.nextgenscience.org/overview-dci

Okun, T. (2021). *White supremacy culture.* https://www.whitesupremacyculture.info/

Plattner, H. (Ed.). (2010). *d.school bootcamp bootleg.* Institute of Design at Stanford. https://dschool.stanford.edu/

Roberts, T., & Chapman, P. (2017). Authentically engaging elementary students in the designed world. *Children's Technology and Engineering, 21*(4), 15–17.

Roberts, T., Maiorca, C., Jackson, C., & Mohr-Schroeder, M. (2022). Integrated STEM as problem solving practices. *Investigations in Mathematics Learning, 14*(1), 1–13.

Wood, M., Sheldon, J., Felton-Koestler, M., Oslund, J., Parks, A. N., Crespo, S., & Featherstone, H. (2019). 8 teaching moves supporting equitable participation. *Teaching Children Mathematics, 25*(4), 218–223.

INDEX

**JENNIFER M. BAY-WILLIAMS,
JOHN J. SANGIOVANNI,
ROSALBA SERRANO,
SHERRI MARTINIE,
JENNIFER SUH, C. DAVID WALTERS**

Because fluency is so much more
than basic facts and algorithms.
Grades K–8

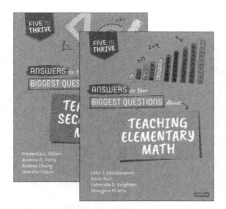

**JOHN J. SANGIOVANNI, SUSIE KATT,
LATRENDA D. KNIGHTEN,
GEORGINA RIVERA,
FREDERICK L. DILLON,
AYANNA D. PERRY,
ANDREA CHENG, JENNIFER OUTZS**

Actionable answers to your most
pressing questions about teaching
elementary and secondary math.
Elementary, Secondary

**ROBERT Q. BERRY III, BASIL M. CONWAY IV,
BRIAN R. LAWLER, JOHN W. STALEY,
COURTNEY KOESTLER, JENNIFER WARD,
MARIA DEL ROSARIO ZAVALA,
TONYA GAU BARTELL, CATHERY YEH,
MATHEW FELTON-KOESTLER,
LATEEFAH ID-DEEN,
MARY CANDACE RAYGOZA,
AMANDA RUIZ, EVA THANHEISER**

Learn to plan instruction that engages
students in mathematics explorations
through age-appropriate and culturally
relevant social justice topics.
**Early Elementary, Upper Elementary,
Middle School, High School**

**SARA DELANO MOORE,
KIMBERLY RIMBEY**

A journey toward making
manipulatives meaningful.
Grades K–3, 4–8

A Sage Company